What the Heck Were You Expecting?

D0029081

What the Heck Were You Expecting?

A COMPLETE GUIDE FOR THE PERPLEXED FATHER

by Thomas Hill

Cader Books

HEARST FREE LIBRARY ANACONDA, MT

THREE RIVERS PRESS • NEW YORK

Copyright © 2000 by Cader Company Inc.

All rights reserved. No part of this book may be reproduced or transmitted in any form or by any means, electronic or mechanical, including photocopying, recording, or by any information storage and retrieval system, without permission in writing from the publisher.

Published by Three Rivers Press, New York, New York. Member of the Crown Publishing Group.

Random House, Inc. New York, Toronto, London, Sydney, Auckland

www.randomhouse.com

Produced by Cader Books, 38 E. 29 Street, New York, NY, 10016, www.caderbooks.com

THREE RIVERS PRESS is a registered trademark and Three Rivers Press is a trademark of Random House, Inc.

Printed in the United States of America

Library of Congress Cataloging-in-Publication Data

Hill, Thomas.
    What the heck were you expecting? : a complete guide for the perplexed father / by Thomas Hill.
      p. cm.
    1. Fatherhood—Humor. 2. Child rearing—Handbooks, manuals, etc.
3. Child rearing—Humor. 4. Father and infant. 5. Fathers. I. Title.
HQ756.H553 2000
649'.1'024—dc21   00-023464

ISBN 0-609-80516-9

10 9 8 7 6 5 4 3 2 1

First edition

For Michelle with all my love. Be prepared.

Acknowledgments

Thanks to Michael Cader for the idea and for his always-fine guiding hand, and to Jonah and Jacob for training him in the ways of fatherhood. Thanks to my critical readers for numerous improvements, corrections and additions: Nancy Burrows, Frank Czuchan, Rick Groel, Adam Idelson, Michelle Piccolo, David Rieth, Kim Rosenblum and Nina Silvestri. And by extension, special thanks to the babies whose crying, idiosyncrasies, smiles, and sleeping habits helped inform this book: Alexandra Lilly Burrows, Samuel Beck Rosenblum, Simon Faber Idelson and Frank Robert Czuchan III. And of course, thanks to my babies, who aren't babies anymore: Deke and Fred. Finally, a tip o' the hat to Jeff Martin, for his unique literary explication of *Pat the Bunny*.

CONTENTS

What You May Be Concerned About
    Giving the Bath
    What to Buy
    Environmental Hazards
    Time to Punt
What It's Important to Know
    Sleeping Like a Baby
What to Be Terrified About This Month
    Driving
Another Thing to Be Terrified About This Month
    The Colic
A Few Things to Say to Let Her Know That You Are Caring, Sensitive
    and Up on the Required Reading

What Your Above-Average Baby May Be Doing
What Your Wife May Be Complaining About
What You May Be Concerned About
    Legitimate Smiling
    When Parents Disagree
    La Donna è Mobile
    Childproofing Your Home
What It's Important to Know
    Facing "The Change"
What to Be Terrified About This Month
    SIDS
A Few Things to Say to Let Her Know That You Are Caring, Sensitive
    and Up on the Required Reading

What Your Above-Average Baby May Be Doing
What Your Wife May Be Complaining About
What You May Be Concerned About
    The Cute Pediatrician
    Taking a Nap
    Sign Language
    Singing to Baby
What It's Important to Know
    Divide and Be Conquered
What to Be Terrified About This Month
    Tuition
A Few Things to Say to Let Her Know That You Are Caring, Sensitive
    and Up on the Required Reading

A Few Things to Say to Let Her Know That You Are Caring, Sensitive
     and Up on the Required Reading

CHAPTER NINE: The Seventh Month

What Your Above-Average Baby May Be Doing
What Your Wife May Be Complaining About
What You May Be Concerned About
     The Advent of Dadaism
     Teething Pain
     Still Not Sleeping?
What It's Important to Know
     Baby Literature
What to Be Terrified About This Month
     Rare Diseases
A Few Things to Say to Let Her Know That You Are Caring, Sensitive
     and Up on the Required Reading

CHAPTER TEN: The Eighth, Ninth & Tenth Months

What Your Above-Average Baby May Be Doing
What Your Wife May Be Complaining About
What You May Be Concerned About
     Drooling
     Circlehead
     Not Enough Information
What It's Important to Know
     Making Baby Laugh
What to Be Terrified About This Month
It's Definitely Your Turn
A Few Things to Say to Let Her Know That You Are Caring, Sensitive
     and Up on the Required Reading

CHAPTER ELEVEN: The Eleventh Month

What Your Above-Average Child May Be Doing
What Your Wife May Be Complaining About
What You May Be Concerned About
     Look Who's Talking
     Mommy's Turn
     Dressing for Baby Success
     Calling the Pediatrician
What It's Important to Know
     Father's Health Issues
What to Be Terrified About This Month
     Unsafe at Any Speed

A Few Things to Say to Let Her Know That You Are Caring, Sensitive
    and Up on the Required Reading

What Your Above-Average Baby May Be Doing
What Your Wife May Be Complaining About
What You May Be Concerned About
    Boredom
    Occupational Training
    The Baby Book
What It's Important to Know
    How to Throw a First Birthday Party
What to Be Terrified About This Month
    Contaminants!
A Few Things to Say If She Still Doesn't Get It to Let Her Know That You Are
    Caring, Sensitive and Up on the Required Reading

What Your Above-Average Toddler May Be Doing
What Your Wife May Be Complaining About
What You May Be Concerned About
    ESPN as Edu-tainment
    Is My Sister's Kid Gifted?
    Taking the Lord's Name in Vain
    Pick Me a Winner
What It's Important to Know
    Toddler Television
What to Be Terrified About in the Toddler Years
    Bad Influences
A Few Things to Say to Let Her Know That You Are Caring, Sensitive
    and Up on the Required Reading

What Your Above-Average Child May Be Doing
What Your Wife May Be Complaining About
What You May Be Concerned About
    Naming Redux
    The Birds and the Bees
    Little League
What It's Important to Know
    The Pre-Rebellion Years
What to Be Terrified About for More or Less the Rest of Your Life
    That You Were a Bad Parent

Foreword

by Samuel Beck Rosenblum

(What better perspective, and what better expertise, than that of an actual nine-month-old to provide the introduction to this book? Rosenblum has enjoyed the world so far, still lives with his parents, and has been described by his grandmother as "very advanced." The following is entirely his own work.)

```
   yvvmb ml msxzzzdee3rrra/lqa4rzaczws
5r44rb      nnmj 'b
 1111;;/
 kkkkmmmkkkkkkkkkkkkkkkkkkkkkkkkkk
fvmtrrrgffffffffv X V UYUYKNK
   SZX?"U7IIIJKM, ,
   NNNB////,
X
```

NNNMN>AAAAAAAAAAA

INTRODUCTION: What the Heck?

Y ou've done it. You've had a baby. The cigars have been passed out, the announcements mailed, the infant bundled up and brought home. You are a father.

You're exhausted; there are a million things to do; everyone is criticizing, advising, correcting; the office called; the baby needs a change; the latest research shows that Mozart does no good for baby's intelligence, but learning sign language does; and by the way have you started saving for college...Augh! Well, what the heck were you expecting? (And yes, "heck" is the strongest word available to you with young ears in the house.)

That's why we've written this book, a guide to parenting that is just for men. A father's experiences in the first year (and beyond!) are unique. They deserve more than a sidebar or appendix in the childcare manuals. During pregnancy, there were lots of books to read. There were reassuring guides to the birth experience, as well as long lists of all the possible complications and medical anomalies. There were childbirth coaching techniques, diet guides, baby name books and more. There were even books specifically about the father's experience.

But giving birth was just the beginning. Being a father is the greatest challenge—and greatest joy a man can face. There is so much to do! For one thing, the woman's role is no longer so obviously more important. Back when she was writhing around screaming how "unfair" childbirth is, there really wasn't much you could do but look sheepish. Now? Well, aside from lactating, there isn't much you can't do. (And science may change that yet!) Yet somehow, you are not given your due. Where are the books for fathers? We hope that this book—no matter how much thinner, cheaper and less informative than mothers' guides—may help to right this injustice. But we recognize that there is a long way to go.

Let's talk about the attitudes of society. What does "mothering" a baby mean? All sorts of care—one envisions feeding, hugging, dressing, clipping the baby's nails. Yes, mothering is sweet and wholesome. Now take the phrase "fathering a baby." Hmm. The image is a little different, right? Who fathered this baby? Another example: Whole stores are devoted to offering a wide variety of fashionable, comfortable maternity clothes, so why does everyone look down on a nice paternity suit?

The point is that society tells us that a father's primary role is biological. In the traditional view his contribution starts as recreation, and continues more or less the same way. He may be the breadwinner, but when it comes to the home, he is inconsequential. He is good for playing with the baby, dependable when a silly dance is needed, more or less the genial buffoon of the family unit. Even traditional roles like disciplinarian, handyman, and preacher of stern moral lessons—the tasks Ward Cleaver, Mike Brady, and Dr. Huxtable did so well—are more and more usurped by mothers.

But today's father is more involved than ever before in the nurturing and care of his children. He even has some advantages over the mother. No matter what the age difference, a man is generally closer in maturity to the baby. Unlike women, men are likely to genuinely enjoy a good game of "peek-a-boo" or a rousing round of "soooo big." Long after Mom is bored, Dad can happily continue to build block towers and knock them down with a big "uh oh!"

Playing happily is a great start, but every father nowadays is expected to be involved and knowledgeable about infant psychology, nutrition, basic medical needs—and, of course, he is expected to change his share of diapers. And because a father today at the dawn of the millennium is not really so different from the detached and repressed career man of the 1950s, he is grossly incompetent at all of these skills. This book will help every father to accept his inadequacies and failings, will guide him in disguising his mistakes and covering up his slip-ups, and will teach him now and then to say the right thing, even if he is not sure exactly what it means. At the very least, it will help him recognize

that he is not alone. It's like a father's support group between two covers, and the best part is, you don't actually have to share your feelings. So read, enjoy, be proud. You're a dad and you love your kids, and truth be told, as long as you make sure they know it, you can't go far wrong. And once a year, you can still go out with the guys, if you play your cards right.

What follows is a road map of the year ahead. In each chapter you will find essays on key topics, a list of baby's developmental stages to look forward to, and a list of what your wife will be complaining about so that you can be prepared. Each chapter also addresses typical fatherly concerns, and highlights one thing about which you will be or should be terrified. Finally, each chapter includes a small section of legitimate advice and information that you can use to impress your wife—and fellow parents, too! These are written in handy first-person format so that you don't even have to rephrase them.

So whatever you were expecting, read on, because *What the Heck Were You Expecting?* can help you prepare for all the things you weren't expecting.

THE USUAL NOTE ON PRONOUNS

The author of any pregnancy, baby or child-rearing guide is always faced by the gender pronoun issue. It's traditional (and sexist) to just go with "he" to indicate a generic infant. "S/he" looks like a mistake. Using "she"—the affirmative action solution—might help make up for years of injustice, and make my feminist sisters happy but frankly (sorry, Catherine and Sara) we just couldn't get used to it. (By the way, the author will be referring to himself as "we" because it sounds a lot more authoritative, and we can use all the help we can get.) (And while we're in a parenthetical mode here: you, too, may find yourself relying on "we" a lot now, as a way of taking credit for all the ideas, planning, and work your wife does.)

In the end, just as we did in our previous work, *What to Expect When Your Wife Is Expanding*, we will be bravely turning tail and fleeing from the issue. Whenever possible we'll use "the baby" instead of any pronoun, and where it's absolutely necessary we'll use the slightly dehumanizing, but gender neutral "its" as the singular possessive form. It may not be the most elegant, but at least it's not *too* sexist. Although, as at least one reader has pointed out, worrying about the pronouns being sexist in this just-for-fathers book may be like rearranging the proverbial deckchairs on the *Titanic*. Enough preamble, you've got a baby to take care of, so get reading!

CHAPTER ONE

Before
the Baby

WHAT YOUR WIFE MAY BE COMPLAINING ABOUT

You're just getting started, but when it comes to complaining, there's not really a ramp-up. What follows is a short list of some possible topics for anxiety, criticism, and general misery. By no means is this intended to be a complete list, and every wife will have her own individual complaints, peeves, and sore points. If your wife doesn't have these complaints, don't worry that she may be "falling behind" or "developmentally slow." Each wife will complain at her own pace, and that's okay.

• Exhaustion

• You

• Her convinction that she has twins, despite all evidence to the contrary

• The fact that there are really ten months of pregnancy, not nine, because one doesn't have the baby until the end of the ninth month, and forty weeks sounds like ten months to her

• Why should a father even get to refer to a baby as "his"?

• The doctor must have figured the date of conception wrong, because the baby feels full-term already

• Who is Braxton-Hicks and why did he invent these contractions?

• Why is it that now that you spend every single night at home watching TV, every prime-time TV show is about people at an earlier stage of life than you?

• She's not sure she's ready for this, and she know you're not

• That if you've driven all the way to the hospital, they should deliver the baby, not tell her that she's not ready

• All this nesting is turning her into her mother too soon

• The dog already looks suspicious and lonely

• You won't stop suggesting terrible names (or the same rejected name over and over)

NIPPLE MASSAGE

"We're going to be breast-feeding the baby, but my wife is anxious because some of her girlfriends had a really miserable time with it. Is there anything we can do to prepare, I mean specifically, I read about, well, certain preparations that might, you know, help."

Nipple massage. That's what you're asking about, right? Sure, there's no medical evidence that this helps prepare the nipples for the rigors of breast-feeding, but she doesn't have to know that, right? Legitimate authorities—we wouldn't make this stuff up—suggest that the nipples be massaged regularly before childbirth. Suckling is hard on them, and once breast-feeding is underway there is no giving them a rest. Just read her the sections about how to take care of sore nipples: try to let them air dry; be careful to break the suction slowly when ending a feeding; and a little lanolin is okay to help cracked skin. Ouch. After hearing that, she'll go along with any stupid idea that might help. As for you, enjoy it. It's sort of a farewell party.

BEING UNCONCERNED

"To tell you the truth, I'm not that worried about becoming a father, the wife seems to have things pretty much under control, and her mom is probably going to show up and run the show anyway. Point is, this book is real cute and all, but do I really have to read it? And do I have to read all these other books my wife brought home?"

So what you're really asking is whether any of this will be on the final exam? That's terrific that you aren't afraid to embrace your classic male indifference. All this talk about "being better than our fathers" was just a load of hooey. Fair enough. No, you don't have to read the book. If you're interested in keeping your wife off your back, you could just skip to the "A Few Things to Say to Show That You're Sensitive..." sections, and if you want to get the basics of baby care and child development maybe you could just catch the next *Rugrats* marathon on Nickelodeon. That should cover you. But you're not allowed to pass this book on to a friend. Everybody has to buy their own. Oh, and as far as warnings and important things you should know: say goodbye to sex, say goodbye to your friends, start saving for college, and buy yourself a nice TV.

What It's Important to Know

BREAST OR BOTTLE?

Once upon a time, as a bachelor, this may have been the choice you faced for an evening's entertainment. Life changes, priorities change. Today, of course, this is the choice between the methods of feeding an infant. It's a debate into which no right-thinking, she-fearing husband would dare interject a real opinion. It's just too loaded with issues about your wife's feelings of inadequacy, femininity, and biological fear. Your best bet is to listen carefully—oh, it's not that hard—and try to agree with her as often and thoroughly as possible.

The fact of the matter is that it is a simple issue. Breast-feeding is the best choice for the baby. For the mother, the issue is mixed. For the father, bottle would be best.

Why? It's pretty obvious isn't it? Those are—were—your toys! Not only are they going to be pretty busy over the next three, six, twelve months—but let's face it, they're not going to be quite the same after all that stretching and suckling.[1] That's not all. If you're using bottles, your wife won't be displaying her breasts in public. She'll actually be able to go to dinner with you once she decides it's okay to leave baby with a sitter (and she can wear a silk shirt without fear of leaking, too). The breast-feeding woman can also suffer from vaginal dryness[2] and sore nipples that can make sexual

1. Not that you will ever, ever admit this.
2. Sorry you had to hear that.

activity difficult. It's nature's way of saying, "Hey, hold it, you've already got a baby!" (Besides, it's extremely optimistic and foolhardy to start thinking about sex already.) Finally, choosing the bottle allows you to be every bit as involved as the mother in feeding the baby, and just as capable of answering the two A.M. siren...wait a second, maybe breast-feeding isn't such a bad idea. Yeah, that's right. After all, it saves money, is more natural, more convenient, healthier for baby and mother—let's face it, breast is best!

What to Be Terrified About Before the Baby Arrives

EVERYTHING THAT CAN GO WRONG

To be really, thoroughly and properly terrified before you have a baby, you need a lot more information than lies within the scope of this thin volume, but we will do our best. We will include a good amount of information and advice throughout the text that will keep you up at night (you need to be waking up every two hours anyway), and we will highlight one topic each month that should get your special, fearful attention.

For this month, think about all the things you don't know and might never find out. If that's not enough, go do some research. There are numerous sources of complete, detailed information that will scare the daylights out of you. Choose a nice thick pregnancy book, and look through the index for things that sound like medical anomalies in newborns. (Just for starters, why not look up undescended testicles, inverted nipples, and the condition where the exit hole is on the wrong part of the penis.) Another good source is the Web, where you can find support groups for every imaginable birth and parenting problem. If you're still not satisfied, try parenting magazines for the very latest possibilities and dangers. Finally, if all else fails, just watch the local news. They'll be sure to have an exposé about your drinking water, your public schools, renegade sex-pervert nannies on-line or some such thing. It's enough to scare anyone.

A FEW THINGS TO SAY TO LET HER KNOW THAT YOU ARE CARING, SENSITIVE AND UP ON THE REQUIRED READING

Bear in mind, these are genuine pieces of information and therefore, not all that funny.

1. "Did you know that the five-part Apgar test that is used to measure the immediate health of newborns—you know, APGAR: Appearance, Pulse, Grimace, Activity, Respiration—was first named for the doctor who invented it, Virginia Apgar, and only later was the acronym created for it?"

2. "The Consumer Products Safety Commission says that crib bars should be no more than 2⅜ inches apart from each other, the mattress should be fit snug within the crib frame, and the top of the mattress should be no closer than 26 inches to the top of the crib railing."

3. "Look at this honey. There's an on-line site, www.babycenter.com, that actually provides a 'sports event conflict catcher' to help 'swinish' husbands—and I suppose, female sports fans—figure out when it would be best to conceive based on avoiding giving birth during such events as the Rose Bowl, Daytona 500 and the Tour de France. Boy, some guys are real jerks, huh?"

4. "Doctors say that sexual intimacy is very important for the health of a marriage."[3]

---

3. It's always worth a shot.

CHAPTER TWO

The
First
Day

WHAT YOUR ABOVE-AVERAGE BABY MAY BE DOING

- Focusing on nearby objects

- Moving fingers, toes, eyes

- Peeing

- Breast-feeding

- Squeezing your thumb with a remarkably vicelike grip

- Being so darn cute that even hardened, cynical, underpaid night nurses coo with delight

- For the sake of physical appearance, going through a complicated, painful, unnecessary surgical procedure (boys only; girls will wait until they are older to have painful surgical work for the sake of physical appearance)

- Looking at you in a way that seems like he knows circumcision isn't medically necessary and is resenting you

- Exhibiting the Babinski, Moro and Palmer grasping reflexes, among others

- Going bald (the full head of hair at birth is often lost quickly)

- Growing accustomed to his name

- Sporting fancy ID band—first fashion accessorizing!

- Passing meconium, and that's an accomplishment

- Relishing newly earned national citizenship

- Making plans on how to drive you crazy in sixteen years

WHAT YOUR WIFE MAY BE COMPLAINING ABOUT

- Exhaustion

- You

- Her convinction that the hospital somehow switched babies

- Why should we have to give this innocent child something as cold and dehumanizing as a Social Security number?

- Circumcision

- Hospital food

- You

- You're not enforcing the "no visitors touching baby because of germs" policy

- The endless snuffles and noises and interruptions of "rooming-in" with baby

- Guilt over not "rooming-in"

- Fear that the name you've chosen isn't working, and that it was you who insisted on it, even though it came from her family

- Your mother

- Her desire never to leave the adjustable recliner hospital bed

- How unfair it is that you won't be able to tell the permanent eye color for months

- That everyone insists on telling stories of labor and delivery that were worse, more complicated or longer than hers when she's just trying to stay focused on how miserable she feels

- The expensive "going-home" outfit for baby is way too big; and the one for mom was way too...optimistic

- You won't steal more hospital diapers

- Everyone else insists on telling her stories of labor and delivery that were easier, simpler and shorter than hers just when she's starting to feel better about her delivery

GOING BACK TO WORK

"How soon after giving birth will it be safe for me to go back to work?"

There is no set timeline that can guarantee a new father's personal safety. Each husband will have to decide for himself, based on his own level of risk aversion. Some may want to simply stay home with their wife and new baby until they are finally asked to go away. Others may choose to check their e-mail from the hospital.

Paternity leave is still a hazy area in many workplaces. It may be a part of official human resources policy, and yet it is perceived of as "wussy" or demonstrating a lack of commitment. Nonetheless, a good basic plan might be something like three days off after the actual birth. Then a week at work while your mother-in-law is around constantly, then take two-weeks "vacation" or "leave" to be with your newborn. Then save some vacation or personal days for "I just can't take it anymore" days during the first four months.

But really the initial question is misstated. The real question is, after you choose to go back to work, how long before it will be safe to return home?

BASIC BABY HOLDING

"Somehow I've made it to fatherhood without ever holding an infant. I've seen it done, but it looks a little complicated. Frankly, I have no idea what to do, and I don't particularly want to ask for directions from my wife."

Whether you ask or not, you will be provided with step-by-step guidance, if not from your wife then from a bemused nurse. The basic theme of these directions (apart from the side comments about how awkward and tense you look) is to support the head. Now don't get excessively focused on the head—the body will need support, too. Do not just grab that head and hold on.

The best way to make your first approach to holding the baby is to imagine that you are creating a tiny chair out of your arm, shoulder and chest. Try to make it a recliner, definitely with a nice headrest. Then you just let Junior take a well-deserved sit-down. (We were going to say "take a load off" but babies are very sensitive about "diaper humor" and might take offense at anything resembling a joke about their incontinence.) After that, it's like holding a nine-iron. Your grip should be firm enough that it won't come loose, but gentle, so as not to crush the baby.

In general, to mix sporting metaphors (but at least we started a new paragraph to give you time to adjust) holding a baby properly is like holding a football—not with your fingers across the laces to pass, but tucked in the crook of one arm to run. The main problem novice infant-clutchers have is that, in their anxiety to use all available resources, they try to make use of both arms. It's not necessary and you end up looking as if you're trying to keep the baby from wriggling free, which will eventually become an issue but not for a while yet. Holding a baby is essentially a one-arm task. The second arm should be able to swing freely to one side, and, with practice, will be able to be employed in both directly baby-related tasks—poking at their dimples, catching spit-up, giving the finger to the answering machine, and signaling your wife to be quiet because you think the baby finally has fallen asleep—and unrelated tasks—channel surfing, playing "air piano" during favorite musical passages, or signaling your wife to come help because you think your arm has fallen asleep.

OPEN EYES

"Our baby is looking all around. I thought that babies were born with their eyes closed?"

That's kittens.

THE MEANING OF LIFE

"Becoming a parent is really intense. I feel like I'm beginning to question everything. Why bring new life into a world where pain and injustice are everywhere? And what does it all mean? Why are any of us here?"

While you're pregnant and in those first days you may find yourself wrestling with such profound philosophical issues. However, you'll soon forget that you were ever troubled by such deep and important thoughts.

Parenthood is many things, but one of its most important functions is shunting aside the existential crises that strike us all. Even if you have found some measure of solace in religious or spiritual choices, you have been through the same process of questioning why we are here and what our role in the great plan is. You've wrestled with the meaning of life. You've been in turmoil over the purpose and validity of your career.

Then suddenly, wham, childbirth and it all has meaning! There's nothing deep or profound about it. You need to take care of this brand new person! Your purpose is to raise and nurture the baby. Your job is to provide for its needs. You live in the present.

Now, having a baby doesn't really address the broader issue of the meaning of life. In fact, there is one more person who will someday realize that they don't know "what it all means." But you're off the hook. Parenthood is sort of a self-perpetuating delay tactic, because after your children wrestle with the meaning of life for a few years, there's a good chance they'll have kids and realize that while the ideas of Sartre, the Buddha and Christianity all offer interesting approaches to meaning and existence, they, like you before them, should really just start focusing on saving enough money to pay their kids' college tuition.

What It's Important to Know

YOUR EMPLOYMENT AGREEMENT

Up to now your primary focus as an adult has been work and career (well, maybe watching pro football and women came first for a while, but now you're probably married), so it may be beneficial to think about your new parental responsibility in terms that are familiar: terms of employment. It is fitting to look at parenthood as a form of employment contract, because while the baby may weigh less than your laptop, that little doughball is your new boss. Meet your immediate supervisor. And don't think that you'll be

able to get away with much, because you're now the direct report of a tiny tyrant. Signing the letter agreement below won't be necessary. You're committed and agreed in whole and in part, in all universes known and unknown, by having the baby in the first place.

EMPLOYMENT AGREEMENT

Dear Dad,

Your new baby ("Baby") having recently entered into a new world at [Insert Name and Full Address of Your Hospital Here], agrees to employ the Mother and Father ("You") and You agree to accept such employment upon the following terms and conditions.

1. Term. The term of Your employment shall commence as soon as Baby does, and shall continue for as long as Baby desires, for a minimum of eighteen years, after which point Baby shall continue to draw upon Your financial resources at will but may choose never to call.

2. Duties. During the employment term You agree to devote Your entire time, energy and attention to the nurture and care of Baby, with the understanding that it may be economically desirable for You to go to work on occasion, although Baby reserves the right to wail uncontrollably when such plans are executed, and resent Your absence to any degree Baby sees fit. The specific requirements and duties that Baby will require may change without a moment's notice for no apparent reason, and furthermore, Baby will not eat strained squash ("Squash"). You may also be asked to handle excrement and vomit on an as-needed basis, and no, lemons don't get that smell out.

3. Hours. You will provide for Baby's care continuously for twenty-four hours a day, seven days a week, every day of the year, making Yourself available whenever Baby makes the following request: "Whaaa!" You are expected to figure out what is desired without further directions. In years to follow these directions will become clearer, but will remain as unreasonable as Baby sees fit.

4. Vacation. You have no vacation from these duties. However, at Baby's discretion, and only insofar as Baby is fully included in all plans, vacation days from your ordinary workplace may be taken after they have accrued to the point where if You don't take one You will lose your mind.

5. Optional Holidays. You have no optional holidays.

6. Personal Days. You have no personal days.

7. Sick Days. Sick days refer to days when Baby is sick and requires your complete attention. Days when you stay home from the office because you are deathly ill shall be referred to as "Extra Help" days, because, as long as you are around, maybe you could help out a little.

8. Compensation. There will be no compensation understood or implied by these terms, although Baby will occasionally begin to smile at You, and later will seek Your approval and love above all others. This affection will wax and wane within a range that is generally consistent with other children, and may be withdrawn without notice at any time.

9. Benefits. There shall be no benefits besides the ordinary tax exemption and the affection described above. Any joy or satisfaction You take from this process is the property in whole and in part of Baby, and should be remembered during future periods of high stress like when Baby is throwing up in the back seat fifteen minutes into a five-hour drive, pitching a baseball though the front-door window, or backing over the mailbox. The foregoing is fully intended to limit Your ability to scream, rant, and set unreasonable limits on desserts, computer time and/or dates.

10. Other Benefits. The above is not intended to set any limit on the number of photographs You take, video or audio recordings You make, and chalk drawings You commission. You may also have all the strained Squash, because, as previously stated, Baby will not be eating it.

11. Noncompete. You are not expected to contemplate having, or have other children who might compete for Your time or attention. Should You choose, nonetheless, to add members to the family, Baby will have the right to engage in sibling rivalry which shall consist of endless rounds of teasing, hitting, claiming superiority and generally attempting to annoy, poke, prod, pinch and negate any or all such siblings.

12. Nondisparagement. You are never allowed to say anything disparaging or critical about Baby, and if You do, Baby has the right to say "You just don't understand" at any time, with the further proviso that Baby may even up the ante to "You don't love me" whenever You are feeling particularly vulnerable.

13. Return of Property. After a period of approximately twenty-one (21) years, exact time to be set at the complete discretion of Baby, one room in the house and Your life will be returned to You in part. Any permanent changes in the color or amount of Your hair, texture of Your facial skin, state of Your back, and/or Your general physical condition is Your problem. You may, however, feel free to keep and store, so long as nothing is ever thrown away without consulting Baby: any accumulated toys, trophies, comic books, Legos, autographed baseballs, dried worm collections, special rocks, computer games and strained Squash that were left behind.

14. Bonuses. On the anniversary of the inception of this contract, (Baby's Birthday) and such religious and secular holidays as are generally accepted in our community, You will be expected to provide an array of gifts, including both items specifically requested and stunning but wonderful surprises. Any disappoint-

ment Baby may demonstrate will rest heavy on Your heart.

15. Equal Opportunity Employer. Baby refuses to admit that You are ever fair or evenhanded, or ever will be.

16. Confidential Information. Baby shall, at any time after his mastery of or partial familiarity with spoken English, feel free to share any information about You that You do not thoroughly hide, with any neighbors, friends or employers as Baby shall see fit, with the understanding that Baby's desire is to get a big reaction. If the material is working, Baby will take it to larger venues. This is in repayment for ever thinking that Baby would eat strained Squash in the first place. Baby shall hold no obligation, either implied or by consent, to reveal when Baby understands English, and further, when Baby can understand the spelling of words aloud, i.e., "Can he have C-A-N-D-Y?" or "I think it's B-E-D-T-I-M-E."

Since the foregoing correctly sets forth our understanding of the terms and conditions You can sign or not sign, whereupon this letter shall constitute fair warning.

Very truly,
and quite literally, Yours,

Baby

THAT YOUR LIFE JUST CHANGED FOREVER

It's fortunate that having a baby takes nine months. This gives a father time to adjust. Rather than just slamming on the brakes, nature provides a long slow deceleration for your life. (Can you imagine waking up after a wild night to "Wake up, honey, we made a baby, he's in the other room sleeping"?)

After you find out that you are expecting, life can seem pretty normal during the early months. There may even be a month or two when the pregnancy is a secret the two of you cherish. Then you go public, a stage in the acceptance process. Later, your wife's exhaustion, choice not to drink coffee or alcohol, slow walking pace, and many other changed behaviors all help you prepare for the metamorphosis ahead. Some theorists believe that the hormonally influenced mood changes are an evolutionary method of preparing the male to deal with the wildly unpredictable moods of a two-month-old.

Still wondering if indeed you should be terrified? Wondering if your life really will change forever? Well, it will. And you have every right to be terrified. But you also have every reason to be overjoyed. Let the wild ride begin!

A FEW THINGS TO SAY
TO LET HER KNOW THAT YOU ARE
CARING, SENSITIVE AND UP ON THE
REQUIRED READING

Warning: Don't read your wife all of these at once. Try to drop them into the conversation casually, to give the impression that you are overflowing with information.

1. "They say not to worry too much about taking pain medication if your doctor recommends it in the first few days. While the drugs can make their way into your breast milk, a nursing newborn is only getting a very small amount of colostrum, and it's worth it to relieve your pain so that you can relax."

2. "I don't see what everyone complains about—it says here that most babies sleep between thirteen and seventeen hours a day! Seems to me that'll leave us with plenty of time to ourselves."

3. "Did you know that at birth, the genitalia of both boys and girls are larger in proportion to their overall body than they will be at any time before puberty?"

4. "Did you know that both right- and left-handed women instinctively cradle their newborn on the left side, with baby's head near mom's heart? And that the heartbeat has been shown to be a calming influence?"

CHAPTER THREE

The First Month

WHAT YOUR ABOVE-AVERAGE BABY MAY BE DOING

• Holding up head

• Sleeping for three- and four-hour stretches

• Establishing a regular feeding schedule

• Responding to having his fingernail cut off too short with a burst of wailing

• Lifting his head from the prone position

• Ruining grandma's silk scarf

• Getting acne (talk about advanced! That's teenage stuff, although baby acne gets the cuter name of "milia")

• Executing bowel movements that require more than four wipes

• Cutting your productivity at work by as much as 40 percent

• Listening with apparent interest while you read aloud Shakespeare (or the newspaper, or a phone book, or the fine print on your Frequent Flier miles statement, but Shakespeare sounds better)

• Driving older siblings mad with envy

• Gathering bacterial germs from the many family members, friends, and complete strangers who insist on their turn holding baby

• Turning two mature, intelligent, fully grown new parents into doe-eyed cooing giggle-pusses

WHAT YOUR WIFE MAY BE COMPLAINING ABOUT

- Exhaustion

- You

- Has convinced herself the baby is hard of hearing

- Sore nipples

- Night sweats

- Mother is leaving too soon

- Mother-in-law won't go away

- State of the baby's belly button stump

- Shape of baby's head

- The name you choose

- If breast-feeding is so natural, why is it so darn difficult?

- Sorry state of late-night television

- Can't help wondering if maybe the other gender would have been better

- Now really isn't a good time for taking on a lot of new responsibilities, after all she just got out of the hospital

- You bought all the wrong baby things; now you have to buy new baby things

- That baby doesn't know her, much less love her

- The house has been so thoroughly childproofed that she can't cook, open drawers or windows, or go to the bathroom

- She can finally look straight down and read the scale again (sounds like a positive thing, doesn't it? It's not).

GIVING THE BATH

"One of these other so-called helpful books suggests that giving baby a bath would be a great duty for the daddy to take on as his special time. Now I'm not against helping out, but I prefer my role as willing-but-fairly-incompetent assistant. Giving an infant a bath sounds complicated, and frankly, dangerous."

Relax. While giving the bath is complicated, and involves hard surfaces, temperature control, and handling a slippery baby, it can indeed be a satisfying task. In any case, it's highly doubtful that your wife will really leave you totally in charge of the activity. She will be there to critique your every move, as usual. Furthermore, even if the actual bathing process can be a little scary for you and baby, there is nothing more satisfying than a freshly bathed, towel-wrapped baby: happy, warm, soft, and smelling a whole lot better than usual.

Another great thing about bathing the baby is that there is none of the tedium of most baby care. There is no sitting and staring and attempting to will the clock forward until the appointed time for you to go "off-duty." When it's bath time, you have a complicated series of tasks to perform. Each part of the baby's body is to be soaped and cleaned. You need to work around the eyes. Shampoo needs to be applied, and rinsed. And you need to accomplish it all while using both hands to hold the baby.

Finally, and most exciting of all, the baby may want no part of it.

At first, all babies will be surprised by the idea of a bath. Some will get to like it pretty quickly; others will resist it for months. Our theory is that to a baby, a bath is reminiscent of the womb and the sensation of being surrounded by amniotic fluid. This could be a pleasant thought (baby's first nostalgia?) or it could actually be scary. "Holy pacifier! They're not planning on putting me back there, are they? Not that it was so bad, but the trip! What a headache!" (Other theorists have put forth the "Lobster Syndrome" hypothesis, suggesting that babies resist the bath because they believe they are being cooked for dinner.)

Luckily, almost every baby eventually learns to enjoy the bath, exploring the sensations of water, the way it feels, the way it pours, the way it can be splashed all over daddy's face and hair and clothes and shoes. They love a classic rubber ducky, especially trying to chew his ducky head off. They'll enjoy floating toys, and holding them below the surface and then seeing them bob to the top. They'll be interested in the warmth of the water compared to the cool air. They'll love the expression on Daddy's face as they decide to pee (or worse) right there in the bath, and enjoy watching Dad drain the entire tub, rinse everything and go through the whole bathing process again! Bath time is fun time!

WHAT TO BUY

"The heck with saving for college, let's start spending. My little baby deserves the best. What can I buy to provide for baby's every comfort and need?"

Put away the Visa card, mister. There will be plenty of things to buy, but you've got to go slow. In fact, by now you've probably already spent a few thousand dollars on a car seat, crib, high chair, mobiles, stroller, running stroller, mountain-bike-stroller, mechanical swing chair, model railroad set, humidifier, backpack carrier, baby monitor, bathtub seat, etc.

Let's take a different approach. What things should you not buy, and why?

• Stuffed animals. These will appear in your home in droves without your ever making a purchase. In fact, it may seem they are actually multiplying in your child's room, but there is no scientific proof of this.

• Cute outfits. Unfortunately, you should focus your spending on the boring essentials, plain white onesies, socks, tees, etc. Relatives and friends get to have all the fun of picking out elaborate French-made outfits.

• Home baby-food grinder. Yeah, right, and you're going to start baking your own bread and growing yogurt cultures, too.

• Anything for yourself. You can't afford it right now.

• Nice clothes for your wife. She'd just get vomit on them.

ENVIRONMENTAL HAZARDS

"Okay, I've checked the home for asbestos, radon, leaking carbon monoxide. We had paint chips tested for lead. I think I've done everything I can, but I can't help wondering if there is something I may have missed."

You've done well, but there is another group of biochemical and environmental hazards that you should address as soon as possible. These are the human-borne contaminants. Each baby will have their own set of potential problems, but just for example, there may be doting elderly aunts whose cheap perfume can overcome an infant. Grandpa's Old Spice can also be a danger. Hyper-competitive brothers-in-law can fill the room with an air of superiority. You may also notice, for the first time, that some of your oldest, dearest friends can't seem to talk without putting an obscenity in every other sentence. It may be okay now, but will they be able to break the habit before your baby starts picking up some salty language?

What You May Be Concerned About

TIME TO PUNT

"I'm looking for some advice about dealing with my wife. Specifically, I've felt totally lost ever since I finished coaching her through labor. See, I was a football player. Still love the game. Is it possible you could help me out with some football metaphors?"

Sure, no problem. Once you have a kid, you are basically playing defense. Your job is to minimize damage, hold the line, plug the holes, and control the line. You'll never have the ball again. In the world of parenting, dads are not "skill players."

What It's Important to Know

SLEEPING LIKE A BABY

Sleep, for those of you who got this book as a gift when Bill and Marcy finally came to see the baby three weeks after it was born, which frankly was annoying because the first weekend everything was in such chaos it didn't matter how many people trooped by and they would have been welcome, but now you're finally trying to establish some sort of regular schedule and the last thing you need is somebody stopping by on the spur of the moment, expecting a drink, some crudités and a cute baby show and frankly...where were we?

Sleeplessness can cause irritability, disorientation, even mild hallucinations. But let's begin at the beginning on this important topic. For those of you who already have a baby, sleep is a period when you close your eyes and become more or less unconscious for a period of time and then slowly regain consciousness when your body is fully rested. Remember that? This "sleeping" traditionally happens at night, for periods ranging from seven to ten hours, less if you want to hit the gym before work. Sleep is recommended by many doctors for relief of common drowsiness and can effectively cure many forms of tiredness.

However, babies hate sleep. They resist it. They wake up unhappy, and they are unhappy when sleepiness approaches. Why is this? Or to put it differently: Oh merciful Lord, please tell us why it has to be this way! Our theory is that sleep is terrifying when you're so new to the world. Put yourselves in baby's place for a moment. You're looking around. It's a lot colder than it used to be. And brighter, too. Faces, noises, smells. You're assaulted by new sensory input. It's fascinating, but worrisome. You're hungry. This is a brand new feeling. You're trying to sort things out, deal with your needs, figure out what's what—and suddenly you start to black out! Things are getting fuzzier. Your body feels heavy. Your eyes keep closing. What is happening!?

You'd resist sleep, too, if, for all

you knew, this was it, sayonara, good-bye, exit stage left, Mommy's breast we hardly knew ye! Of course this theory doesn't explain why babies cry even more when they are waking up. Perhaps they're dreaming of a better place, where food is brought directly to your tummy through a tube, it's always warm and soft all around, and there is a dependable lub-dub sound effect that's got a beat you can really dance to.

Whatever the reason, babies are grumpy going down and grumpy getting up. (Maybe the problem is the idea of "going down." That does sound bad. We have to put the baby down. What's going down? This baby, that's what! I'm gonna put the baby down. Baby, you're going down!) The most immediate impact baby's resistance has is that you, as the parent, will not be sleeping for any longer than the baby. As the old joke goes: How'd you sleep? I slept like a baby—woke up every two hours and cried!

What to Be Terrified About
This Month

DRIVING

You've been doing it since you were sixteen. (Even longer if you count taking Billy Grosvenor's dad's Pontiac to the end of the street.) It's second nature to you. You've logged hundreds of thousands of miles. And then, it all changes. You get behind the wheel again, but this time your little bundle of joy is strapped snugly into an approved car seat in back. Your child is now depending on you for its very life.

Suddenly the very idea that people climb into two-thousand pound metal boxes and hurl themselves from place to place depending only on their hand-eye coordination seems foolhardy. Even if you were never a defensive driver, you are now aware of each impending possibility. "That guy sees us, doesn't he? Why is that guy tailgating me? If I accidentally turned the wheel four inches to the left, the car would fly over the embankment within seconds." It may even cross your mind that you are being propelled forward by a series of explosions of gasoline in compressed metal cylinders and it is totally unclear to you how that could possibly be safe.

With time and experience, your fears will subside. You'll be able to drive without anxiety. In fact, you may discover that a drive in the car is one of the only sure ways to get your baby to sleep. Sure, it's easy for the baby not to worry. For them, a car is just a giant vibra-bed that doesn't even require quarters!

Just remember what they always say, statistically speaking, driving is much safer than flying in a plane. Oh, wait a second, that's not what they say; it's the opposite that is true. Oops. Well, don't worry anyway. At least when you're driving you can choose to drive safely, and no oxygen mask will ever drop from the ceiling.

Another Thing to Be Terrified About This Month

THE COLIC

Not everyone refers to this condition with the definite article. Some people talk about "babies with colic" and even "colicky babies." But those 20 percent of all parents, the ones who have truly experienced it because 20 percent of all babies have it, describe it with the full formality it deserves: The Colic. There is crying, fussiness, discomfort, and The Colic. You know, as there are colds, but there is "The Flu."

The worst part of it is that there is so little you can do, so little doctors know, so little sleeping going on. Basically, at about two or three weeks of age, some babies get The Colic. It might be indigestion, but whatever it is makes them cry, inconsolably and frequently. You can walk them, burp them, swing them, pat them, put on a little vaudeville show. Eventually they will sleep (because all mammals require sleep to survive) but always less frequently and for shorter periods than other babies. They cry and they cry. They don't hate you, it just seems like that for two or three or four months.

Are there cures? Sure. There are folk remedies like a drop of water from dew gathered on the night of a full moon. There are diet adjustments you can make: a dairy- and wheat-free diet for Mom has been suggested. Some parents have found that baby will calm down when lying on top of a vibrating washing machine during the spin cycle, but that's a major waste of electricity and water.

Are there any positives? Yes. In fact there are two. First, you will have boasting rights at the playground when new parents are comparing their misery. Second, eventually, it will end. You don't see a lot of colicky tenth graders, after all. But in the meantime, your baby has The Colic. And when baby has it, the whole house has it. And yes, crying can be contagious.

A FEW THINGS TO SAY TO LET HER KNOW THAT YOU ARE CARING, SENSITIVE AND UP ON THE REQUIRED READING

1. "Even in the first week of life, it's been shown that infants are able to distinguish the smell of their mother's milk from other mothers' milk. Smell is one of the earliest ways that babies recognize and attach to their mothers. See, maybe 'Fido' wasn't such a dumb suggestion for a boy's name, after all?"

2. "You know it may sound strange, but I read that, when you're giving an infant a bath and accidentally get soap in its eyes, the best way to remove it is to lick it out. All these dog parallels...I wonder if we can just spread newspaper out on the kitchen floor?"

3. "According to the *American Journal of Psychiatry*, 3 percent of fathers shows signs of experiencing their own postpartum depression. Among the factors contributing to their state of mind are: being older, daunting responsibilities, a shrinking social network, and a volatile or decaying relationship with a partner. Whoa. Honey, is my social network shrinking?"

4. "Listen to this one. Statistics show that attendance at work is better among married men with children and spikes even higher among fathers of newborns. Quite a coincidence, huh?"

CHAPTER FOUR

The Second Month

WHAT YOUR ABOVE-AVERAGE BABY MAY BE DOING

- Rolling over

- Smiling

- Smiling with a little half-curled upper lip like Elvis

- Paying attention to small objects

- Combining two sounds—"goo gee" or "gah goo" or even "gee gah"

- Bringing hands together

- Accepting the fact that going back to the womb is not an option

- Expressing fashion preferences: soft things with big neck holes are so, so "in"

- Expressing a clear preference for Mom over anyone else (sorry Pop, Grandma, Aunt Martha)

- Insisting on four complete outfit changes a day

- Burping like a truck driver

- Seeming to achieve a regular sleeping pattern and then, for no discernible reason, having a total relapse to the completely irregular sleeping pattern of the first weeks

- Saving all the diaper action for when Daddy is on duty

- Sucking the thumbs or fingers, especially while going to sleep

- Sucking the thumbs or fingers, especially while Daddy is going to sleep but can't because he is trying to figure out how he'll be able to pay the orthodontist

- Stating emphatically and clearly that he does not agree with the "let them cry it out" school

WHAT YOUR WIFE MAY BE COMPLAINING ABOUT

- Exhaustion

- You

- Has convinced herself that the baby will need glasses

- That walking a baby outdoors seems to give complete strangers license to critique her parenting

- If life were fair, babies would smile right away (and maybe even come out saying "thank you" and "I love you," too)

- Baby's bellybutton is definitely an outie

- Her own bellybutton still hasn't returned to its prepregnancy state

- Sitting around at home all day with no interaction with adults gives her way too much time to think about things like bellybuttons

- That the closest she's come to a fashion statement lately is a cloth diaper draped fetchingly over one shoulder

- Just got the pictures back, and believes there should be legislation to protect new mothers from having their picture taken for at least forty-eight hours after giving birth (some recent mothers have suggested as long as four months would be fair)

- The only tavern in walking distance doesn't allow strollers

What You May Be Concerned About

LEGITIMATE SMILING

"All right, our son's face does a lot of different things. Some of them could definitely pass for a smile in my estimation. Naturally, people are always telling me it's just gas. So how can I know for sure what's a real smile? The baby book is waiting for a precise date."

What we prefer to answer to skeptics is, "Of course it's gas—that's why he's smiling!" It shuts them up at least. But the truth is that it may not be easy to tell when the first social gesture is truly attempted. After all, those first smiles are little experiments. They are a cause and effect. Baby smiles—and your face lights up, you coo, you pay more attention. Baby might not realize the connection at first, but through trial and error it will begin to understand that its smile is a powerful weapon. And when baby has truly mastered the smile, you'll forget all about the little twitches, sneers, and pouts that you stared at hopefully for that first month. You'll drink it up. It's about as good as a facial expression can get.

What You May Be Concerned About

WHEN PARENTS DISAGREE

"We've always had a good relationship, but with the baby fraying our nerves it's hard to be polite and make the effort to work things out. Worst of all, we seem to have two very different parenting styles. We're constantly at odds about how long to let the baby cry, how much strangers should hold him, what he's ready for. The question is, what happens when my wife and I just can't come to an agreement over a specific issue?"

In such a case, she's right. She's always right.

What You May Be Concerned About

LA DONNA È MOBILE

"I'm sorry, I know it helps her get to sleep, and it's fun to watch the little clowns circling above her, but it can't be good for my daughter to listen to the 'Love Theme' from The Godfather *over and over and over. It's not that song in particular; it's any song. Even an infant must want some variety."*

When it's getting tedious for you, your baby is just beginning to enjoy the predictability. After all, so little in a baby's experience is predictable. Babies have no information, no assumptions. Put yourselves in their booties. Imagine going through a day where every single event is basically a complete surprise: "From sleeping, you slowly become aware that a square box with red figures is beeping at you and now your eyes are opening and, holy cow, there's bright light coming in those wall-rectangles!" No wonder babies sleep fifteen hours a day!

So the short answer is that it's practically impossible for a baby under the age of three months to get bored with a song. But if you feel it's important, a little variety can be provided by simple rotating the mobile with others. However, this won't provide a very wide range. Here are some of the songs commonly found on wind-up mobiles:

"Rock-a-bye Baby"

"Twinkle, Twinkle Little Star"

"Lullaby Baby"

Bach's "Minuet #3"

Mozart's "Eine kleine Nacht musik"

"Lara's Theme" from *Dr. Zhivago*

"Round the Mulberry Bush"

"Zip-a-Dee-Doo-Dah"

Now, if we lived in a perfect world, someone would make baby mobiles with a much larger variety of songs. After all, even if the kid doesn't get bored, we've got an extremely tired adult in the room patting his back over and over desperately hoping for some sleep. Here are some songs that would be fine choices for wind-up mobiles (and would also make a nice compilation tape for long car trips, by the way):

SIDE A—For Baby

"Tonight the Bottle Let Me Down," Merle Haggard (and that next line? "and let your memory come around")

"(Let Me Be Your) Teddy Bear," Elvis Presley

"In the Wee Small Hours of the Morning," Frank Sinatra

"Folsom Prison Blues," Johnny Cash (Okay, maybe there are some questionable lyrics, but no song better communicates the desolation of languishing behind bars!)

And, of course,

"Stuck Inside of Mobile with the Memphis Blues Again," Bob Dylan

SIDE B—For Mom and Dad

"Stop Your Sobbing," The Pretenders

"Get Back," The Beatles

"Sleep Baby Sleep," Jimmie Rodgers

"Baby Please Stop Cryin'," Bob Dylan

"Wild Thing," The Troggs

And finally,

"La donna è mobile" from Verdi's *Rigoletto*

Of course, this is all well and good, but ignores the real issue of mobiles. But you must learn to accept the fact that the mobile makers have conspired to prevent the music from playing for more than two minutes, which frankly is very seldom enough time to lull any baby to sleep. You must then go in to the room, and noisily crank the key for thirty seconds, basically setting the whole process back to square one. If they can put an entire sonata into a greeting card, why can't they create a ten-minute mobile?

What You May Be Concerned About

CHILDPROOFING YOUR HOME

"Some of our friends are making us feel bad because we haven't child-proofed the apartment yet. But our baby is only a month old. What's he gonna do? Trash the mobile?"

When it comes to childproofing, the tendency is to overdo it, and to do it sooner than you really need to. Now, it's true that erring on the conservative side isn't a bad idea. One mistake can have nasty consequences. But locking down the toilet lid when you're only six months pregnant is overdoing it. (And after all, since your wife is now going every twenty minutes, it's hardly worth locking.) Our advice is to wait. Childproof not just after the baby is born, but after the baby starts to get mobile. It's like the story of the architect who built a group of buildings with a central courtyard. The construction crew asked where they should put the sidewalks, and he told them not to put in any. They made it all lawn, and after six months the architect returned and said, "Put the sidewalks where the paths in the grass are worn." (It's an instructive story, and the fact that he was sued for breach of contract by the angry construction company and residents who had been walking through mud for six months, is really beside the point.) So where were we? Oh yes, we weren't childproofing until after the child has created a path of destruction through your home. No, no, that's wasn't the point at all. The point of our little parable of "The Architect, the Angry Tenants, and the Hedgehog" (I left out the part about the hedgehog because it wasn't relevant to child-proofing) is that it is easy to get suckered into every gimmicky safety precaution ever invented. Just take care of the basics: cover the outlets, move breakable objects out of reach, put the sharp-edged coffee table in the basement, and childproof any kitchen or bathroom cabinets with potentially dangerous or messy items in them. You'll also want to move everything of real value into deep storage in another state. After that, follow your baby's lead. If they're fascinated by flushing things away, go ahead and get the lid-lock. If electrical cords are irresistible, buy the special covers. If they keep biting the cat, buy the "My Lil' Muzzle."

It's not as if you're going to run out for a quick round of golf while the kid wanders around looking for trouble. You're going to be watching, and the trouble spots will make themselves apparent. Of course, all this is coming from a man with an entire shelf worth of hard-cover books whose slip covers have been carefully peeled off the spine, and who, furthermore, actually did lose a VCR due to a Mickey Mouse key chain pushed in the tape slot. So maybe you're better off using your own judgment, and not mine.

What It's Important to Know

FACING "THE CHANGE"

People used to talk about changing diapers as if it would be a miracle if a man could, or would, manage it. All that has changed, of course, and men are now expected to do their fair share. (And likely more, since they can never really compensate their wife for the pain, trauma, and self-sacrifice that is childbirth.) With the prospect of changing diapers, new fathers still may be intimidated by the warnings from older generations, or doubtful females: "I can't wait to see *you* changing diapers!"

Then the baby arrives, and the new father discovers that changing diapers is nothing. It's a piece of cake, to use an unfortunate metaphor. You're likely to wonder what the fuss was all about. The baby needs a change, you whisk them to the changing table, off goes the old, a couple of handy premoistened baby wipes—wax on, wax off—maybe a little powder for style points, flip out the new diapers, tuck, tape and done. Frankly, figuring out how to rebutton or resnap the outfit is the toughest part.

So what's the big deal? First of all, you're at two months, buddy, you ain't seen nothing yet. Sure, it's not the "mustard" (sorry, but that's the word every advice book uses, and who are we to break with tradition?) of the early weeks, but more changes lie ahead. Solid food. Raisins. Lima Beans. Over the next eighteen months, you'll become intimately aware of the causes and effects of the developing digestive tract. You'll learn which things manage to pass through the entire system relatively unaltered. We're not going to tell you, either. It's better to be surprised. Just a couple things to keep in mind. First: corn. Second: getting all the way through your commute, into the office, and through two meetings when you suddenly realize that your hands smell and why.

But even that doesn't really explain why people used to think a man was incapable of changing a diaper. Why was it? The fact is that it never used to be this easy. You've been saved by modern technology, mister, as the marketers and innovators of the hygiene industry strive to protect our sensitive modern souls from everything that is dirty, messy, germ-ridden or unpleasant. You're probably using disposables, most people do. These little miracles of modern science practically change themselves! They absorb liquid so effectively you may not even be able to tell a diaper is wet except for the change in weight. They are built to fit, and stay on unless you really botch it. The tapes hold—but come off and go back on if you need to adjust them. The dirty diaper wraps into a neat little self-sealed unit to be tossed away. Incredible.

Cloth diapers are the reason that changing diapers was once so feared. Just twenty years ago, they were still the norm. Turning a rectangular cloth into a serviceable diaper—on and staying on—requires two safety pins, a little origami, some familiarity with basic wrestling holds, a relatively squiggle-free infant, no fear, and three hands. Even this is easier today, because the environmentally devoted parent who chooses cloth gets to use Velcro diaper "wraps" to hold the cloth in place. Only the hopelessly out of date are still actually using diaper pins and rubber pants. It was pins and folding and tucking that built up the legendary stature of "diaper changing" as something to be feared, and rightfully so. A man facing a diaper change in 1970 was likely to stick the infant hip with a pin, or emerge with the diaper bunched all in front, or back, or off to one side—or most

likely of all, to watch the diaper simply drop off at the first wriggle.

The reputation of diaper changing will probably never recover, but the truth is that today it's easy. The man facing a diaper change in the year 2000 is accomplishing a feat that ranks, in pure level of difficulty, well below flossing your teeth and only a little above making a paper airplane. So go ahead, change the diaper. You get more credit for it than you really deserve. Maybe you'll even get to see a ball game again.

What to Be Terrified About This Month

SIDS

There's certainly nothing funny to be said about Sudden Infant Death Syndrome, but it's just as certainly a fact that you're going to think about it. After all, it's the reason you won't sleep well the first night that baby sleeps in another room. It's why, on that wonderful day that baby sleeps through the night, you'll think, "Wow, he slept through the night" for all of one second before you think, "Oh, my God, he hasn't woken up yet?" Maybe it's God's way of giving you one small reason to be happy when you're awakened for yet another four A.M. feeding.

Blessedly, SIDS is a very rare occurrence. The latest advice is to encourage infants to sleep on their backs, on a firm mattress, with no pillow. Research is still underway, so you should consult your pediatrician for the very latest advice.

What happens if your baby simply won't fall asleep on its back, but happily snoozes the minute it turns tummy down? Now what are you supposed to do? Are you willing to ignore the latest dictums, just for the sake of some shut-eye? You have entered what is known as the "pancake" stage. You let the baby fall asleep face down, and when it seems to be safely approaching REM sleep, you carefully flip it onto its safer side. Naturally, the baby wakes up. We didn't say it would work, did we?

Perhaps we can't stop you from all your nightmarish supposings on this issue, but try to get over it. There are so many other things to worry about, you don't really have time to obsess about this. Another idea is to divert your fears. Focus on fearing alien abductions instead. At least that way you'll keep it to yourself and your online *X-Files* buddies.

A FEW THINGS TO SAY TO LET HER KNOW THAT YOU ARE CARING, SENSITIVE AND UP ON THE REQUIRED READING

Those readers who are bored by real information can now move on to chapter 5, where the comic observations will recommence.

1. "For the first six months of life, a baby's vision is blurry, no better than 20/40. Babies are, naturally, somewhat better at seeing close objects, while distance clarity comes later. See, I told you he doesn't need glasses."

2. "When babies are being undressed, they will sometimes complain, crying and then crying even more when they are completely naked. They're not shy, or cold—they've just become accustomed to the feeling of clothes, and any change becomes discomforting."

3. "Scientists have established that the ideal rate for rocking a baby to sleep is about sixty rocks per minute, and the side-to-side movement should be about three inches. This is about the pace you get from natural walking—which may be the reason it is appealing to the infant. It emulates the pace they experienced in the womb."

4. "Did you know that, according to some doctors, the number-one cause of colic is the breast-feeding mother drinking cow's milk?"

CHAPTER FIVE

The Third Month

WHAT YOUR ABOVE-AVERAGE BABY MAY BE DOING

- Smiling

- Chortling

- Holding head steady when upright

- Grasping a rattle

- Grasping a baseball (why not start now?)

- Bearing weight on legs

- Reaching for something

- Sleeping through the night (it could happen)

- Grasping the difference between night and day, and not caring

- Saving you a bundle in taxes

- Waiting to pee until the diaper is off, just for the sport of it

- Attempting to nurse and suck a thumb at the same time

- Coming up with at least one symptom, behavior or problem that does not seem to be addressed in any of the books

- Developing a diaper rash that can make you wince just to look at it

- Refusing to give up the pacifier

- Developing gross motor skills (as well as gross movement spills)

- Developing a complex, emotionally resonant relationship with the nice person at the table who keeps looking back and forth and is, in fact, an oscillating table fan

WHAT YOUR WIFE MAY BE COMPLAINING ABOUT

- Exhaustion

- You

- Anything she can think of

- Has convinced herself that the baby is bow-legged

- If God gave men nipples, why don't they have to breast-feed, too? (don't try it, it hurts)

- Her hair loss (it comes out in handfuls after the pregnancy hormones wear off)

- Baby's hair loss (the hair at birth is often quickly shed)

- Your hair loss (hey, you're not nineteen anymore)

- That sweat pants aren't considered fashionable

- That her old clothes are mocking her

- Just thought of a better name

- Has become convinced that the electromagnetic field generated by the baby monitor is a health risk

- There has got to be a more humane way to catch mice

- Accidentally spoke "baby talk" to the FedEx delivery man

- Can't believe it, but it's official—she no longer cares how the house looks

- That you came home with an "off-road stroller" with independent four-wheel shock absorbers, light-weight titanium frame, and a roll-bar

- Sudden worry that carrying the baby is making her upper arms look too muscled

- Can't hear the TV well when she's eating pretzels

What You May Be Concerned About

THE CUTE PEDIATRICIAN

"I'm not the jealous type, really. But the way my wife talks about the pediatrician, it's like he's George Clooney, T. Berry Brazelton and Mel Gibson rolled into one. Should I be worried?"

Women with new babies often go through a stage that is known scientifically as conjugal malabsorption syndrome, or more colloquially, as not being able to stand you anymore syndrome. For most husbands this change is a small one, and they may not even notice the difference. For others, the increased irritability, lack of affection and frequent questioning of their competence, honesty, and/or fidelity can come as a shock. The cause of the syndrome is simple. Parenthood is a major stress and taking care of a baby has a tendency to highlight everything that was wrong with the husband in the first place. Being lazy, self-absorbed, messy, and insensitive can only be accentuated by the increased workload, number of needy humans, household chaos and raging hormonal imbalances.

Furthermore, the typical male was once able to get away with a lot of dysfunctional behavior because, after all, he was a guy, and guys do that. In fact, it was kind of cute when you tried to clean the entire living room carpet with a lint brush because the vacuum cleaner bag was full. However, a sea change has occurred. There is no longer a need for cuteness in the house. That role has been usurped by the new kid in town. You can't compete, so be prepared: "Can you please do something useful?"

This is all to say that the most frequent result of conjugal malabsorbtion is that other men become much more appealing. The cute pediatrician is the prime candidate for these shifting emotional needs. He knows all about babies. He answers her endless questions patiently. He even gave her his phone number the first time they met. If your wife's pediatrician is female or looks more like George "Goober" Lindsey than George "Dr. Ross" Clooney, then her efforts to seek out suitable replacements for you may take other directions. Other men at the park, especially stay-at-home dads, are particularly appealing because they are so "naturally nurturing." And, as always, firemen have their own special appeal. Luckily all this is unlikely to lead to a sexual dalliance, since that would involve sex, and for all intents and purposes, that's out of the question. After all, she's not likely to forget what got her into this mess in the first place. So don't worry too much. In almost all cases, a woman's relationship with her pediatrician is nothing more than a harmless infatuation.

TAKING A NAP

"I understand that during this period, nap time is very important, and that it should be as regular as possible. But it's hard to hide from my boss long enough to get a decent nap."

Napping is important. Don't forget that there are many cultures, especially in southern climes, in which an afternoon siesta is a regular part of adult life. However, many employers are quite ignorant of world culture. This does not preclude the possibility of a nap, it just means you may need to be more creative.

Option one, if possible, is simply to close the door to your corner office, pull the shades, and have your secretary hold your calls. That may not work for all of you. What about the health club? You may already belong and there may be a nice quiet corner where you could do some "yoga" with your eyes closed. A nice long bus ride can be restful—just spend your lunch hour going to the end of the line and back. A park bench can be nice in season. If you become attached to sleeping out of doors, you can try sleeping over heating grates during the winter, but you may be given free sandwiches by local housing authorities. It's a risk you may be willing to take.

SIGN LANGUAGE

"I understand that some behavioral psychologists recommend teaching babies sign language. What's up with that?"

They are entirely serious. The underlying idea is sound. Even very young infants have a desire to communicate, which comes well before the ability to form sounds and words with the mouth and vocal cords. By teaching them hand signs to ask for specific things, you satisfy that need and make your parenting that much more efficient.

However, we believe that this is ultimately a fad that will pass quickly, like teaching infants to swim, or piping Mozart into the womb. Teaching a baby to sign is great, except that you have to teach yourself the signs first. Furthermore, once a baby can use sign language, how much will they really have to say? "I'm hungry" and "I'm uncomfortable" and "I'm scared of Grandpa" and that's about it. All things that good old-fashioned crying already communicated pretty well.

Finally, this is fresh science. Who knows what the long-term effects of learning sign language are? One could imagine it could retard the natural language learning process. Perhaps babies who sign will mature faster? Or be more prone to carpal tunnel syndrome? They thought teaching babies to swim was a great idea until they realized the infants were drinking a gallon of pool water every time they went for a dip.

SINGING TO BABY

"I've never been much of a singer, but I can't resist making up little songs while I'm trying to quiet the baby. The problem is that my wife thinks I'm going to make our baby permanently tone-deaf because I'm never on-key."

Singing badly is better than not singing at all, and there is no evidence to suggest that a lack of tunefulness will have any impact on your baby's future musicality. If anything, exposure to music of any sort and quality will increase baby's emotional attachment to such sounds.

Furthermore, singing dumb songs is one of the great joys of parenthood. There's so little else to do when you're walking and joggling and trying to use your voice to somehow soothe the little sleepless one. Make up any old thing. It's never too dumb for baby. He's never heard Moon and June rhyme before! However, no matter how sprightly and clever you consider these occasional late night compositions, it's best to keep them to yourself. You'll be surprised how flat they sound in the cold glare of daytime. And besides, no one with the possible exception of your spouse really wants to hear all the words of "My Little Max, Saves Me Tax," "Got Me a Baby Named Mavis, She Prefers to Rent from Avis" or "Dietrich, Dietrich, What a Neat Trick."

DIVIDE AND BE CONQUERED

As you know, if you have read this far, the mother's primary role is to nurture the baby. The father's primary role is...well, he doesn't have a primary role. His is a secondary role. He's the second-string, the relief pitcher, the pinch-hitter. Now perhaps there are some men for whom this is an overstatement, but we can certainly agree that in general, moms are the experts while dads are the able and willing assistants. There's no reason why it couldn't be reversed, now that the baby is out in the open and you both have equal access, but the nine months in which it was obvious that her role was primary have established patterns of behavior and expectations. Actually, who are we kidding? She's always been the boss, always has been, always will be, so let's just move on.

The point is that you can feel left out by her obviously superior parenting skills and instincts. You could try to compete. You could read all the "real" advice books, correct her bathing technique, and suggest a better system of getting baby to understand the difference between night and day, but it may only cause additional strain on your relationship. Taking on separate and complementary roles, while never entirely fair, can be the ideal way to maintain peace, harmony and baby.

How should these roles and responsibilities be divided? Let's look at an ideal situation. You're a working father. Your role is to show up at home as soon as possible after work, be kissed, handed an ice-cold martini and the day's interesting mail, and be presented with a clean, happy, well-rested baby who looks just like you, while dinner is being finished in the...Oh sorry, just got caught up in the fantasy. Start again.

So your role is to show up at home as soon as possible after work, be told that it wasn't soon enough, be handed a pile of bills, reminded of three things that need to be done, and be handed a sticky, napless, pungent baby who looks more like Winston Churchill than ever, while she heads off for a bath—"gotta have five minutes' peace"—with dinner, apparently, a scattering of Cheerios served with partially gnawed and air-browned apple slices.

So maybe the role of the basic working dad is not all glamour, but even with all the juggling tasks, lack of respect, exhaustion and unending demands—and don't tell any women we told you this—it's a helluva lot easier than being a stay-at-home mom.

What to Be Terrified About This Month

TUITION

When you first have a baby, the awesome responsibility can be overwhelming. Your life is changed. You're not sleeping. The light at the end of the tunnel is eighteen years away. Then you realize that's not a light...you're heading straight for the white-hot inferno that is college tuition! It's the all-consuming flame! Those eighteen years are nothing when you consider raising the $200,000 you may need to pay for four years of college.

Perhaps you're already filled with the deep dread that you will not be able to provide your children with the education that has become a necessity in contemporary America. Tuition terror can strike at any time, but for many it happens in the third month of baby's life, when maternity leave is almost over and your wife starts hinting that maybe she won't go back to the office. After all, paying for daycare or a nanny eats up a lot of the money she would be making, and not commuting saves money, and you could start taking your lunch in instead of eating out.

Whether she returns to work, or stays at home, you will someday face the unpayable, immutable, mysterious, looming monster of tuition. Talk to a financial planning expert soon, or take some of the following sensible tips.

- Play the lottery regularly

- Invent and patent something that everyone needs

- Rent out your house and live on the streets for a few years

- Get promoted to president or CEO of your company

- Sell all your worldly possessions and put all the money in a mutual fund; then go door to door asking for alms

- Train your child in some obscure sport for which scholarships are offered, and competition is scarce: fencing perhaps?

- Become a college professor (they are often given big breaks on tuition and other expenses)

- Stay on the straight and narrow now, but start planning now for "the big score": just one major bank heist (or two if you have two children)

- Move to an extremely unusual place, in hopes that colleges will accept your child and provide financial aid to meet their "geographic distribution" quotas (Wyoming or Antarctica might work)

- Do not discourage your kids from studying or participating in school, because no matter how terrible their grades are, there will always be some college that will accept them (and your checks)

A FEW THINGS TO SAY TO LET HER KNOW THAT YOU ARE CARING, SENSITIVE AND UP ON THE REQUIRED READING

By the way, don't let your wife know that you get all your information from this book. The idea is to pretend that you have been reading bits and pieces of all the many books she brought home from Barnes & Noble.

1. "Breast-feeding doesn't ensure that you won't begin to ovulate. Generally speaking, nursing mothers find that they will begin to menstruate again around the time the baby starts on solid foods, or is sleeping through the night. Your body's ready, whether you are or not."

2. "Some bottle-fed babies will actually become obese, generally because their formula isn't being mixed correctly—it's too rich—or from additional foods in the diet. And there is some evidence that obesity at this stage can lead to obesity later, so be aware that chubby cherubs might not be ideal."

3. "When you hold an object out for a three-month-old, let the baby work out how to reach for it. The process of looking, judging, reaching is how it learns. Don't think the baby is getting frustrated and put the object in its hand. It just takes a baby a long time to figure out how to reach for something."

CHAPTER SIX

The Fourth Month

WHAT YOUR ABOVE-AVERAGE BABY MAY BE DOING

- Doing a baby pushup: raising chest pushing up with arms

- Reaching for something

- Using legs to stand up, when you provide the balance

- Turning in the direction of a sound or voice

- Making a raspberry sound (Bronx cheer)

- Making a raspberry sound that can't really have been—but sure seems like it was—timed as a statement of derision

- Helping support the price of Kodak stock through sheer cuteness

- Visiting the outside world

- Blatantly disregarding the clearly printed warnings that objects "may present a choking hazard"

- Preferring not to get "tied down" and "hemmed in" by such a bourgeois notion as a regular sleeping schedule

- Eliminating magazines, entertainment, dinner out, a coffee on the way to work, compact discs, and HBO from your monthly "budget"

- Eating some solid foods (it's very European to start this early, and European babies all seem to know foreign languages so they must be smart—on the other hand, they start kids on red wine pretty early, too, and we wouldn't recommend that)

WHAT YOUR WIFE MAY BE COMPLAINING ABOUT

• Exhaustion

• You

• Has convinced herself that the baby is gay, not that there's anything wrong with that, but she's sure you're not going to be able to deal with it

• Baby hasn't accomplished one of the things on the "What Your Above-Average Baby May Be Doing" list

• And somehow, it's your fault

• The dawning realization that a minivan might actually be a necessity

• The charm of being thrown up on is beginning to fade

• That you actually thought you might start going to your old poker game again

• After all the years of restraint from drugs and alcohol, apparently all her brain cells are being destroyed anyway by the nefarious combination of sleep deprivation, babbling to a baby all day, and a lack of contact with other adults

• That you came back from the grocery store with "Rice Krispies" which, gentlemen, is not what is meant by "rice cereal" (just look for the pictures of babies on the boxes)

• Agrees that the baby should have a sibling; but has not agreed on whose body this one will come out of

• Finds it difficult to keep track of weekdays and weekends

• Three months' maternity leave is not nearly enough; Europe is so much more civilized, and did you know that mothers are given public support just for caring for their children?

What You May Be Concerned About

CHOOSING A NANNY

"The time has come. My wife is going back to work and we need to hire a nanny to take care of the baby. For some reason, the responsibility for this seems to be in my hands. What do I do?"

Don't worry. While many working mothers will, at first, put their husband in charge of arranging child care, they will eventually relent and do it themselves. The initial decision is based on the general principle of "who is that other adult who keeps hanging around and why isn't he doing anything" combined with generalized guilt. Few mothers really want to go back to work, no matter how exhausting mothering can be. The three-month-old, (or four- or five-) is just starting to get really satisfying. So rather than face the fact that listings need to be read, research done, and phone calls made, young mothers will pretend that they will let their husbands figure it out.

But they will relent. Whether a daycare center, a nanny or a relative, the mother will realize that she cares deeply about who is taking over her responsibilities and more or less take over the selection process. All you need to do is make the initial effort and then sit back and wait. "What do you mean she seemed nice? How nice exactly? You didn't ask if she knows infant CPR? Did you call her references yet? Did they seem at all hesitant? Oh forget it, I'm gonna do the next interview."

What You May Be Concerned About

MOVING THE BABY OUT OF THE BEDROOM

"Okay, I only have one question. What's that little bedroom down the hall with the teddy bear motif for? I remember painting it three or four different shades of blue to get the color right. Put up that strip of wallpaper with the teddy bear alphabet on it myself. There also seems to be a changing table and a tiny bed with bars around it. Any idea?"

Okay, we get the point. Your wife still won't let you take the bassinet out of your bedroom at night, right? It not easy to make the transition, but usually after a couple of months or so it's a good idea to establish the idea that nighttime sleeping happens in baby's own room. Sure, it's convenient to have the baby nearby for those frequent nighttime feedings, but you'll also hear every snuffle and whimper. You'll probably all sleep better if you push for separate accommodations. Yep. You in the garage.

What You May Be Concerned About

AMUSING YOURSELF

"We're having a little standoff. When I'm talking or singing to the baby, I sometimes, just to amuse myself, say things that might be considered a little inappropriate—I figure the baby has no idea what I'm saying anyway. My wife is sometimes amused, but also wants me to quit."

What exactly are you saying? Dirty limericks? It's probably not a great idea to get in the habit of using language you wouldn't want to hear your toddler repeat to company. It is, on the other hand, very important when you are talking or singing to a baby that you should feel free to make jokes or references that are "over its head." Why? It's our belief that language and communication skills are best taught in a context that is rich and meaningful to the teacher. In other words, rather than talking down to a toddler or baby, it is important to speak in a way that is relatively natural. (For further discussion, see *"Blue's Clues* versus *Sesame Street"* in chapter 12's "Toddler Television" section.)

In other words, you could sing "Twinkle, Twinkle Little Star" over and over to your baby. He won't get tired of it. He will probably enjoy the repetition. But you won't—and that matters! You should be interested and actively engaged as much as possible. If that means singing "Girl from Ipanema" or "Tangled Up in

Blue" or "Heartbreak Hotel" then you should do it. Yes, your wife may chide you for singing sexist, dark or otherwise "inappropriate" lyrics, but the baby will appreciate the obvious interest you take in these songs. He doesn't speak English anyway, so what does he know?

The same principle goes for made up songs or banter. Let's say you're spoonfeeding the baby. Is it so wrong to try to amuse yourself (and your spouse) by describing each spoonful as something horrific? "Okay son, now I'd like you to taste human flesh, all us zombies love it." Sure, it's inappropriate. Shouldn't joke like that in front of a toddler, but, hey, babies don't care. Singing a made-up song while trying to get baby to sleep? Lyrics about "babies who don't sleep enough have to go work fourteen-hour days in the shoe factory to support their mom and dad" are fine. Whatever it takes to amuse you is okay in our book. Your wife may say it's sick; we say it's a healthy outlet for frustration.

What You May Be Concerned About

TAKING BABY'S TEMPERATURE

"I think we bought the wrong kind of thermometer."

Sure you did. When we were babies, rectal thermometers were the only thermometers. You probably have some dim childhood memory that led you to purchase a "baby" thermometer. They still sell them; they still work. However, there are numerous superior choices nowadays. Why spend any more time than necessary getting up close and personal with your baby's heinie? There are thermometers that can measure body temperature from the ear, armpit, and forehead. By next year they'll probably have a baby monitor that in addition to audio, can provide a constant readout of temperature, diaper moisture, Ph-balance and REM.

Plus, you'll know when your baby has a temperature. Unlike adults, babies can get a very high temperature and still be within normal ranges.[4] A handy rule of thumb is that if you can fry an egg on your baby, that's too hot.

What It's Important to Know

MAKING ADAPTIVE INCOMPETENCE WORK FOR YOU

You've probably already discovered Adaptive Incompetence (AI) by yourself. It is not something most men need to be taught. It's a survival technique that evolves naturally in

4. Please check with your pediatrician or a real baby advice book for exact numbers.

childhood to greater or lesser degrees depending on other psychological attributes of the person. Put simply, Adaptive Incompetence is the system by which work or responsibility is thwarted by demonstrating an inability to effectively accomplish that work. As a child, it is the learned behavior that if your attempt to clean your room actually makes *more* work for Mom, she will be less inclined to make you clean your room. In men, a common example would be that the less able you are to cook a decent meal, the less likely you are to be called upon to cook one. If you thoroughly screw up the laundry and dye beloved clothes pink, you may never be trusted with laundry duty again. If you are unable to successfully change a diaper, you could, *theoretically*, get out of changing more diapers. This is, of course, pure theory. In practice, it is far more difficult to accomplish. Allow us to provide some guidance.

Masters of AI know that it must be employed strategically and passively. The moment there is active incompetence—that is, the moment she (and we use the pronoun "she" for obvious reasons, although certainly the basic theory could apply to nonmarital situations) knows you are doing it on purpose—the entire enterprise is at risk. Furthermore, AI has the property of noninverse erosion: each time you are caught in an apparent active use of AI makes it that much less likely you will get away with it again. Just remember, a good relationship may be based on honesty and trust; but real relationships also include discretion in the mix.

Each new father will have to test

the limits and possibilities of AI in his own relationship. No two situations are alike. It would be foolish for a pastry chef to pretend he couldn't make dinner; or for a mechanical engineer to fob off the crib construction. But vice versa? Might work. Here are some basic tactics and tips to get you started.

1. Sincerity Is the Key
Don't express doubts before you begin. Key phrases at the inception of the task: "Sure Honey, let me take a crack at it." "How hard could it be?" "I ought to be able to manage that."

2. Modest Failings Work Best
Diapering the baby's head is too obvious; better to accidentally tear off the self-stick tabs and then try to repair it with duct tape, because it seemed like a shame to throw out a basically good diaper, and then putting on so much tape that the diaper can't be taken off again without the use of scissors. Overwatering the plants so that water spills over is good; watering things that obviously aren't plants is too much.

3. The Big Flub Can Work, Too
It's more dangerous to pull off, but a single screw-up of epic proportions can become a sort of "relationship legend" that will be quoted and embellished and recalled over and over again. If you can live with the humiliation, it can get you out of a lot of work. "Remember the year he cooked a turkey with the plastic bag of gizzards still inside?" "Oh sure, you're gonna fix the VCR...Do I have to remind you of the great ceiling fan debacle again?"

4. Demonstrate Your Willingness
Never doubt yourself. Better to say "I learned my lesson, I can handle it." As soon as you say things like, "Gee, I don't know, I'm not so good with toasters"—well, methinks the lady will see that you doth protest too much. The power of AI is that it is all about your partner making the choice to actually prevent you from being helpful. "No, no...I'll put it together, you just...uh, go entertain the baby or something."

5. Don't Get Caught
You have to make incompetence a way of life. That demands dedication. One well-prepared omelet, or getting the computer printer to work right, or getting baby to get back to sleep...and bingo, all your hard work at failing will be down the drain.

6. Don't Really Do This
This book is a work, primarily, of comedy. The AI concept—while a true reflection of male behavior—should not actually be attempted. It won't work, trust me, and the possible results are so horrendous that we simply had to interrupt the flow of irreverent wisecracks to warn the tiny minority who might not recognize the very real danger of such an effort.

LOUD MUSIC

Here's a scary thought. You were blessed with a healthy baby, and then, just to indulge a whimsical desire to listen to Boston's "More Than a Feeling" at the same volume you did back in college, you have damaged the hearing of your infant. How much of an idiot are you?

Now don't get too paranoid. After all, that first Boston album just begs to be played loud, and so do Beethoven's symphonies (although look what they did for him!) The fact is that anyone can suffer some hearing loss from prolonged exposure to volume levels that may not even seem uncomfortable. Furthermore, babies' ears are more vulnerable than adults. Play music, but why not keep it in the range of naturally occurring sounds? A good benchmark is that if your wife has to make hand signals telling you to turn it down, or flashes a knife, it may be a tad too loud.

A FEW THINGS TO SAY TO LET HER KNOW THAT YOU ARE CARING, SENSITIVE AND UP ON THE REQUIRED READING

1. "While we're keeping track of the baby's immunizations is a good time to review our own, honey. The Centers for Disease Control recommend boosters for tetanus and diphtheria every ten years, and mumps and measles can be harmful diseases in an adult. Adults can also get a vaccine to ensure they won't get chicken pox."

2. "Periods of amnesia are actually quite common in new mothers, both during pregnancy and after. Though there is no cure, it is generally at a low level of simple forgetfulness and will pass with time. It is somewhat more common in women suffering postpartum depression, or other forms of stress."

3. "We're supposed to keep track of baby's immunizations, but you know that we should also review our own. According to the Centers for Disease Control, we should get tetanus and diphtheria boosters every ten years, and should consider vaccines for mumps and measles, which can be harmful diseases in an adult, and possibly get one for chicken pox. No, I don't think I told you that already."

CHAPTER SEVEN

The Fifth Month

HEARST
FREE
LIBRARY
ANACONDA, MT

WHAT YOUR ABOVE-AVERAGE BABY MAY BE DOING

• Complaining when you take something away

• Sitting without help

• Standing while holding your hands

• Standing while you basically support the arms, legs, and torso, so that you can say that your baby is already standing.

• Getting food (or anything) from hand to mouth

• Talking a long string of nonsense (this is a natural skill at first, which is then lost and can only be regained later by attending college)

• Sleeping through the night (or not)

• Executing bowel movements that require as much as four to six wipes

• Emptying a spout cup with no help (not necessarily drinking any, though)

• Showing interest in what you're eating, and showing a growing suspicion that it might be better than the plastic rattle he's been gnawing

• Losing interest in basic peek-a-boo and demanding more elaborate entertainment before being willing to bestow a smile on the entertainer

• Enjoying a good swing at the park

• Loving the great taste of spoon; but not understanding why you keep taking it away

• Perfecting the classic forty-minute power nap: long enough to revive, too short for adults to accomplish anything

• Taking off the bib whenever he happens to feel like it

WHAT YOUR WIFE MAY BE COMPLAINING ABOUT

• Exhaustion

• You

• Baby's birthmark that was supposed to fade but hasn't

• That she has forgotten what she was just saying

• Yes, you said she looked fine, but she obviously doesn't look fine, so just as obviously you don't even care what she looks like anymore

• That the baby thinks that the baby-sitter is "Mommy"

• Every time she starts to complain, you say, "Boy, this book really has you women down to a tee"

• That Susan Lucci's winning an Emmy kind of took away from her mystique

• *Parents* magazine is significantly less interesting than *Glamour*

• The way you looked at her just then

• Thought that her inability to nap well wasn't going to come up again after she got out of kindergarten; but now it has again become a serious liability

• They were baby gifts, so shouldn't the baby have to write the damn thank-you notes?

• That the baby has begun to resemble your ugliest relatives

• Dawning realization that she may never see her prebaby weight again, but she's keeping that entire closet full of clothes anyway and don't you dare say a word

What You May Be Concerned About

FERBERIZATION

"So we had finally decided to get serious about our baby's sleeping and do this whole Dr. Ferber let-them-cry-it-out thing. Notice I did say 'we' but in practice, she's making me the enforcer! I don't want to be the bad guy."

Think of it this way. You want to sleep, right? If you stick to the plan, use the stopwatch and don't lose heart, eventually both you and your wife will be sleeping through the night. And you'll be the hero! It may not exactly be fair, and it's definitely sexist, but this system fulfills both your needs. By complaining to you that it all seems so cruel, your wife is easing her own guilt. By playing the General Patton role, you get to take credit for being strong and decisive. And after all, while you're sitting outside the nursery door at three A.M. with a stopwatch, what every couple needs is a little added tension.

What You May Be Concerned About

THE KEYS TO DISTRACTION

"I've discovered that no matter what the situation, I can distract our daughter with my key chain.

I'm not complaining, but can you explain it? And will the magic wear off?"

Is it the shininess? The jingling sound? What is it exactly that makes a ring of keys so darn fascinating? Shine and jingle are part of it, no doubt. A ring of keys is a veritable feast for the senses! Visually appealing, aurally stimulating—and tactile, whoa! The cool, smooth feel of metal, and the little sharp-edged teeth. Furthermore, the whole thing is a mass of unpredictable behavior just begging to be studied. You grab part of it, the rest slides away. You grab that part and the whole thing slides back around. It's full of surprises. Last, but not least, this is a unique item in the baby's world. Baby spends lots of time with cotton, plenty with stuffed animals, no shortage of rubberized and laytex covered surfaces, plastics and laminates, cardboard, paper, and lots of wood. But how many things can baby play with that are jagged metal? Or even metal? Saw blades? No. Stapler? No. Pliers? No. Forks, coins, fingernail clippers? No, no, no. The keys are it. It's the forbidden fruit of infantdom.

Of course, skeptics say that keys have become popular only because it's the one thing that a totally unprepared dad is carrying with him that's of any interest at all. Freudians have another theory, but it would only make you feel uncomfortable, so forget we mentioned it.

In any case, one easy "homemade" toy is a ring of real metal keys. (It goes without saying that you'll want to watch them in use—can't have babies poking their own eyes, or yours.) Why should you give baby a set of its own? To save yourself the pathetic ordeal of distracting, pleading, and otherwise trying to extract them from your progeny: "What about Mr. Monkey, don't you want to play with him? Oh look, it's a noisy castanet, what a funny sound. Oh please, please...Daddy needs his keys or he can't drive his car to work!"

What You May Be Concerned About

ZEN AND THE ART OF SPOONFEEDING

"Maybe we started in on the solid foods too soon. He's interested in the food, but not particularly in eating it. I've tried the airplane spoon. I've tried showing him how I eat it. Is there something I'm missing?"

For those three or four months after a baby has started eating solid foods, but before it can use a spoon, the average father will spend a full 20 percent of his waking hours holding a spoon in midair with a dab of rice cereal on it. It is the most tedious, thankless, unending task in all of fatherhood. Babies love it. It is all a big game, and a fun one, too. Take a bite, seemingly in the mouth, but then spit it out. Demand more! Demand the spoon, then fling it.

Grab the food. Squish the food in your fingers. There are infinite possibilities.

Your patience will be sorely tested, but it is being tested now to prepare you for the road ahead. The unending "Why?" game. The "Are we there yet?" The "How many times do I have to ask you to put your shoes on when we've got to go." Try to focus on the spoonfeeding as spoonfeeding. Find your center. Think equanimity. You are superdad. You cannot be phased. Be the spoon!

Finally, don't get in the habit of opening your mouth as you bring the spoon toward baby. It's easy to do. It's sort of a nonverbal signal, a hint to baby that he should open his mouth. But through sheer repetition you will soon find that you do it every time you feed the baby, even when he is perfectly hungry and needs no encouragement. How will you know that you've picked up this unconscious habit? Your wife's snickering is a good hint. In severe cases, you may not be aware that you are slowly opening your mouth as you hand a memo to a coworker, or when you pay a tollbooth clerk. Just another occupational hazard of fatherhood, but best avoided if you possibly can.

What You May Be Concerned About

GOING OUT

"Have I got everything?"

Well, let see. Do you feel like a pack mule? If not, you've forgotten something. Actually, even if you do feel like a pack mule, there is probably something you've forgotten, or never thought you would need.

Have you got a full diaper change kit, with as many diapers, wipes, Desitin and bags for used diapers, as you will need to get through the maximum number of changes possible in the time allotted before you will return to home base for provisions? Do you have enough food? Bottles? Backup bottles? Backup snacks in the event of a spill? Do you have a full outfit change in case of said spill? Do you have sufficient pacifiers, teething rings, interlocking plastic rings, or soft creatures? Or are you up to sand toys, shovels, buckets, cars, ride-ons, balls? Do you have blankets and sweaters for temperature changes? Stroller rain cover? Swiss army knife, for, well, anything. Do you have your cameras (still and video) in the event of an incredibly cute moment? Pen and paper in the event you need to jot down something you would otherwise forget? Cash, in order to buy any of the above, rather than returning home and having to admit that you went out without something you needed? Quarters, for the payphone, or your cell phone and/or pager. Do you have something to read in the event that baby falls asleep on your chest and you're bored silly with nothing to do but stare at the pigeons? Is it small enough that you can manage turning the pages with only one free hand because otherwise you'll wake the baby?

What You May Be Concerned About

HOW HIGH TO TOSS?

"Is tossing a baby okay? I've seen it done, and it sure looks like fun. Now my wife read somewhere that I shouldn't toss the baby at all. I thought it was a classic rite of fatherhood?"

It is. Have no fear. Advice books will always err on the side of caution, for liability reasons if nothing else. But saying that you can't ever toss a baby? Ridiculous. However, there are sensible ground rules you should follow. The first ground rule is don't let the baby hit the ground. In other words, if you're going to toss the baby, you had better catch the baby. (Hitting the ceiling is no good either.)

Also, you shouldn't toss a baby who doesn't have complete head control. There is a danger of whiplash in little ones, but by six months, most babies will have built up the necessary neck muscles. You'll also be able to tell if your baby is ready, because he will let you know if he is not enjoying it. Begin with simply lifting the baby slowly up into the air above you. Then try it a little quicker. That might be enough for a baby under nine months. Then, if you're feeling confident, you can let go and "catch some air." Grab the laces! Firm grip. Full extension. Follow-through!

Now don't feel guilty if you *don't* want to toss the baby. It's natural to be reluctant. And if Uncle Mike is being wilder than you like, tell him so. You shouldn't have to worry about something ridiculous like having baby dropped. There are plenty enough legitimate worries. In any case, you may not want to toss your baby now, or ever, and that's okay. By the same token, a little safe tossing isn't reason to have the authorities revoke your fathering license.

What It's Important to Know
DESIGN FOR BABY LIVING

Many people have wondered why it is that certain motifs dominate the design of items for children. Clothes, blankets, wallpaper, diapers, nasal aspirators—if there's room for a cute koala or a trio of helium balloons, the marketers will put one on there. Apparently these are very powerful symbols. Perhaps it is as simple as using these cultural clichés to indicate to consumers that the item is intended for babies.

"Wow, look at the tiny toothbrush. Why would anyone want a toothbrush that small? Oh wait, it's got a farm animal on it, must be for a baby."

"Boy, I took aspirin, but it didn't make a dent in this headache." "You didn't look on the label, did you? See? A monkey in a baseball cap. Must be for kids."

However, clichés become clichés because they have symbolic meanings. The most common motifs are farm and zoo animals (especially bears and lions), the clown, balloons, fruits (and some legumes, especially peas in a pod), basic geometric shapes, isolated letters and numbers, hearts and flowers (primarily for girls), sports equipment (yes, primarily for boys—don't blame me, I didn't design the stuff!), and of course the logos and or names of college and sports teams.

Why have these elements become so universally accepted as appropriate designs for infants? Some of them are self-consciously aspirational. "Yale, Class of 2021" is not that hard to analyze. The same goes for the future all-stars sporting tennis racquets and "Green Bay Packers" or "Daytona 500" shirts.

The basic geometric shapes, letters and numbers are educational, the parents' way of saying that the baby may be sitting there drooling, but rest assured that every effort is being made to stimulate his burgeoning mental capacity.

The fruits and vegetables are directly related to our primitive desire to ingest our children. "I'll eat you up!" is the theme of many an adult-child interaction during the period where the infant is still smaller than a pot roast; once the baby grows larger, parents tend to move on to other games.

Hearts, flowers and other distinctly feminine outfits are more practical, their goal is simply to help strangers choose the proper gender-specific compliment when they coo at your child: "Oh what a handsome...I mean darling, little baby."

The animals are far more interesting. Even here, at the dawn of the twenty-first century, man seems to have retained an innate belief in animism, the primitive cultural idea that eating a certain animal will imbue us with the qualities of that specific animal. This animistic streak, now buried deep in the subconscious, still surfaces at times. It is our theory that this is why our children's clothing and environment are covered with animals that have seemingly very little relationship to our everyday experiences. What are the tenets of this modern animism? Let's look at it animal by animal.

First, there are birds, whose power of flight symbolizes liberation and possibilities. Cats and dogs symbolize companionship and loyalty. Lions and tigers are symbols of courage and assertiveness. Frogs and turtles, well, they're just really cute. And finally, there are the bears. How many of us have actually seen a bear in the wild? Yet, above all other creatures, it is the bear that has become the most common motif in children's toys, clothing, decor and literature. For a while, some theorists put forth the idea that the bear symbolized a desire to steal a picnic basket from right beneath the Ranger's nose, but that work has been discredited. Today, after much

research and analysis, we have finally hit on what we believe is the reason for the bear's predominance. For contemporary parents, the bear is a symbol of sleeping. We'd like our babies to hibernate. All right, perhaps not hibernate, but sleep a *little* more deeply and thoroughly— like bears. What better decoration for flame-retardent 3–6 mos. onesie pajamas?

What to Be Terrified About This Month

DADDY'S TURN

An associate of ours, whose name will not be mentioned to protect the innocent (although he's not *that* innocent, but that's a different story, and in fact a somewhat more interesting story than this, but there's a time and a place for all things, hope you understand) had an epiphany regarding his role as the father in child care. It is a simple but eloquent truth of having a baby: It's always Daddy's turn.

This may seem an oxymoronic phrase. Doesn't "turn" imply that someone else will be alternating with you? In most situations that is the case, but since Mommy is on-duty all day, working incredibly hard, actually birthed this creature, and has more important things to do, whenever Daddy is available, it's his turn. Even if she has already returned to a full-time job, which sort of evens the score, come six o'clock, she can still use the who-carried-the-baby?-you-owe-me-forever argument whenever she chooses.

Now if you're really tired, have a headache, need to make a phone call, or feel like you've changed enough diapers for one weekend, it is possible—in the literal sense—to declare that it is "Mommy's turn." However, the authors and publisher of this book cannot take any responsibility or liability for the consequences of such an action.

A FEW THINGS TO SAY TO LET HER KNOW THAT YOU ARE CARING, SENSITIVE AND UP ON THE REQUIRED READING

You know, if you really were caring and sensitive, you would read all the real baby books cover to cover. (Just a reminder to make you appreciate these concise tidbits.)

1. "Often infants this age, who are experimenting with the sounds they can create with their mouths, will happen upon sounds they like and repeat them over and over again, happily mesmerized. But if you think that's annoying, wait until your toddler starts to play the 'asking why' game."

2. "You can overcome the baby's stranger anxiety by giving the new person something to hold that's familiar to baby, a favorite toy for example."

3. "You know you're not actually supposed to use baby powder. It doesn't prevent diaper rash, because you need to use something that is a barrier to moisture on the skin, like an ointment. And babies can inhale talcum powders which can lead to lung irritation or pneumonia."

CHAPTER EIGHT

The Sixth Month

WHAT YOUR ABOVE-AVERAGE BABY MAY BE DOING

• Looking for something he dropped

• Passing an object from one hand to the other

• Sorting blocks by size

• Clearing his throat

• Paying a visit to the colleagues at the office, where, through sheer cuteness, he accelerates the ticking on half-a-dozen biological clocks

• Drinking from a spout cup

• Pouring every drop out of a spout cup

• Attempting to set the indoor distance record in the "Spout Cup Toss" event

• Reaching a level comparable to adults in odor-to-body-weight ratio

• Becoming amused by his ability to twist and wriggle while you are trying to get a diaper, sweater or snowsuit on

• Attempting to subsist entirely on Cheerios and apple juice despite your best efforts to vary his diet

• Getting bored with tedious mouth-based eating and attempting to ingest food through osmosis

WHAT YOUR WIFE MAY BE COMPLAINING ABOUT

• Exhaustion

• You

• Being forced to be a working mother

• Being trapped at home as a stay-at-home mother

• The completely inconsistent and incomprehensible sizing systems on baby clothes or your inability to understand the perfectly simple sizing systems on baby clothes

• They warned her about giving up her body; but no one told her about giving up her mind

• Your baby daughter doesn't have enough hair to hold a barrette

• That soap operas are totally inane, a complete waste, and take so long to watch

• That feeding the baby dinner in the bathtub is not acceptable as a handy time-saver

• Still resentful that you never managed to get announcements sent out

• Signed up for a baby massage class and it turns out that the baby is the one who gets the massage

• Somehow the commercials on cable play at twice the volume of the shows, which never fails to rouse the almost-back-to-sleep baby

DO I LOOK FAT IN THESE PANTS?

"I'm no idiot, I know the answer is 'No, you really don't, honey'—but lately, she won't take no for an answer. She's persistent. She'll rephrase the question. She'll try asking in roundabout ways. Help me!!"

Don't give in, be strong! Just say no. Don't hesitate, don't pause—look (you have to have *some* credibility), but don't consider. The answer is no. The answer is she looks great. The only question is "Have you lost some weight?"

The period of time with a new baby, and the long recovery from childbirth, is one in which your wife's self-image is under siege. She's sleeping little. If she's nursing, she's not allowed to go on a crash diet. If she's home from work, she has easier access to snacks than she's had in a long time. The one-spoonful-for-you-one-for-me system of feeding baby can be a dangerous game. All in all, it might be a tough period. That's why the questions come more persistently. But she is not looking for objectivity or reality, she wants to know you still like the way she looks. And you do. Believe me, you do.

What's more, the desperate need for reassurance can lead to a heightened sensitivity. The unwary husband can easily be lured into slip-ups. You're watching some swing dancers, the guy takes a petite woman and flings her in the air. Don't say: "Yeah, it's easy to throw *her*." Seems obvious, but it's easy to let your guard down. Frolicking in the ocean, you pick her up, and say: "Hey, it's salt water, I can carry you all day." Your spirits will not be buoyant for long.

DRUGS FOR COLDS

"Our daughter has her first cold, and the pediatrician suggested medicine, but we're concerned about using too many drugs."

Yeah, but most prescription cold medicine, or even over-the-counter stuff, will have the side effect of having your baby sleep longer. Enough said. (But no pretending you think baby has a sniffle just to get a full night's sleep in. That's cheating.)

THE BIRTH MYTH

"Lately when we meet other new parents and start talking, the wives compare notes on their birthing experience. Here's the thing: every

time my wife tells her story, the labor becomes longer, the nurses crueler, and the complications more terrifying and rare."

Do not attempt to correct your wife on any of the details, or compare her storytelling to "a fish story." Sure, you may have been there, and in a significantly clearer state of mind, but you don't have the right to take anything away from her trauma. For many women, telling the story of their child's birth is a kind of ritual that keeps their visceral bond to the child alive. Like any story that is often retold, the literal truth is not important, the symbolic truth is what she is telling the world. Besides, all women suffer from some degree of amnesia about the birthing experience, so it's natural that they would fill in the missing gaps in the way that fulfills a psychological need.

Other wives may have the opposite experience. Their birth story is more and more happy as it is retold, with less and less effort, until finally she walked to the hospital, told the doctors when she was ready, and the sheets didn't even get messy. For women whose birthing was relatively uneventful, this is another approach to competing with other women at the playground. They become a kind of earth mother, for whom childbirth was as natural as sneezing, and about as uncomfortable. She does not want her image of the birth corrected either.

THE CONCEPT OF OBJECT PERMANENCE

"I'm confused. I've been reading up on all the stages of child development and I don't think I understand the idea of 'object permanence.'"

Object permanence is really quite a simple concept, but interestingly enough, it is one that takes an infant some time to master. All it really means is that things remain in existence even when you can't see them. When babies see a ball bounce behind the couch, as far as they know—since they haven't grasped the concept of object permanence—the ball no longer exists and, to the baby, it is absolutely fantastic that Dad can create another ball just like it by reaching under the couch. It's why peek-a-boo is such a fascinating...

"No, no, I understand all that about what a baby learns. My problem is that lately, with getting so little sleep, and the house being in such chaos, the principles of object permanence don't seem to be holding true."

Ah yes, now we see what you were getting at, and you are correct: the laws of quantum physics do not apply to a home in which a child under the age of six resides. Things no longer remain in existence. Sometimes they simply disappear. You put them down. Turn around. Wham, they have ceased to be. This strange phenomenon is especially prone to happen to small objects of great importance— keys, paychecks, ID cards, fountain pens—although socks, blankets, bottles, favorite toys, books and magazines have also been known to defy the ordinary rules of physical reality and suddenly fail to meet the rather minimal criteria of "existing." However, you may be able occasionally to perform a miracle and reach under the couch and find the I.D. card that you already had replaced. But don't count on it.

What It's Important to Know

BABY SCIENCE 101: NOTES TOWARD THE UNIFIED THEORY

To bond with your baby, it is vital that you understand how a baby thinks. It may not be easy, but you've got to keep one step ahead of your six-month-old. The key to understanding babies lies in recognizing that their primary task during these early years, beyond the basic survival skills, is to analyze and comprehend how the world works. They are sci-entists. Furthermore, you should recognize that as a parent you are not a fellow scientist, a lab assistant, or even a great teacher. You are part of the experiment. You are one of the prime subjects of observation and study. Luckily, we were recently able to uncover and translate one baby's lab notes, giving us a rare glimpse at the workings of the six-month-old mind. Though incomplete, these brief passages give us some insight into the workings of the pretoddler mind.

Day 171. Despite my best efforts, the eye-closing still happens. Sometimes when my eyes are closed, soft-face-mama and scratchy-face-mama go to great lengths to rearrange things. How do they darken the sky, change their clothes, and move all my things in the mere moments that my eyes are closed? Idea: try to avoid eye-closing to catch them in the act.

Day 173. Today, I continue my exploration of the idea that the ground sucks things toward it. When you release food it rushes toward the floor. It is still possible that food can rush to the ceiling, but my efforts to explore this idea have led to my food being fed to brother-plastic-can.

Day 178. Brother-plastic-can must not be touched because he is dirty. He is always hungry and will eat anything.

Day 179. Scratchy-face-mama is sometimes sucked down to the floor. Standing must be tiring, and when he is no longer able to resist the ground, he gets pulled to it. Today I saved him from a bout of eye-closing by pulling the eyes open. This gave him the energy to stand again.

Day 187. A new theory: breast-feeding is a secret soft-face-mama and I keep to ourselves. She covers me when I am feeding and when I try to pull away what is covering me and breast, she is quick to replace it. This is especially true when we are in the bright room with no walls. My hypothesis is that there isn't enough for the others. (Scratchy-face-mama seems to know what is going on, perhaps he just isn't hungry.) Now if the others knew, they would want some, too. Secondary hypothesis: I am, therefore, the single most important being in the entire world. All seventeen of the others in existence must rank below me.

Day 191. The furry baby is a fantastic crawler! I must learn to better use my tail...

What to Be Terrified About This Month

PHOTOGRAPHIC FLASHES

Some Native American cultures reacted to the concept of photographic images with great trepidation. Anything that captured a person's likeness so realistically was bound to be capturing some of their inner spirit, and inner spirit is some-thing you want to hold onto. If there's any truth to the theory, contemporary babies' inner spirits probably don't even make it out of the hospital.

Those first days are just the beginning. How many pictures will you take in an effort to capture that first smile? Ten? Twenty? Fifty? All with double or even triple prints so that all the grandparents are well supplied? Then it's a little late for this information, but guess what? You actually can hurt your baby's eyes with flashes that are too close or too intense. The risk is extremely minimal, but you should keep flashes four feet or more away from their eyes, and even better, if your camera allows it, bounce the flash indirectly or diffuse it. Using natural available light is another option, of course. Remember, the chances of actually having done any damage are slim. Still petrified? Guilty? Good.

And by the way, at least your second child won't have any problems. Since they never get their picture taken.

A FEW THINGS TO SAY TO LET HER KNOW THAT YOU ARE CARING, SENSITIVE AND UP ON THE REQUIRED READING

Listen, if you're still expecting this section to be anything but dry information, you haven't been paying attention.

1. "At six months, babies will begin to distinguish between reality and things seen in a mirror. They will look behind them if your image shows up in their mirror, where once they might have reached 'into' the mirror."

2. "Babies' initial babblings actually sound the same all over the world. The distinctions among language groups comes later, as the parents repeat back to their baby the parts of their babbling that sound like elements of the language they speak."

3. "At this age, a baby may begin to focus on a single 'transitional comfort object' that can become a very important part of your lives—the animal, blanket, or soft toy that becomes the necessary companion, especially for any trips out of the house. If such a 'talisman' is adopted, smart parents might want to create a duplicate (buy another of the same bear, or even cut the blanket in half) so that they will be covered, so to speak, when the crisis of the lost or misplaced item arises."

CHAPTER NINE

The Seventh Month

WHAT YOUR ABOVE-AVERAGE BABY MAY BE DOING

• Picking up tiny objects

• Pulling itself up from sitting to standing

• Doing a baby sit-up—getting into the sitting position from lying down

• Clambering toward objects of desire

• Calling you by your "title"—mama or dada

• Putting one object inside another (i.e. a ball in a cup, or your car keys in an open floor grate)

• Sleeping through the night (however, neither the author nor the publisher can in anyway be held liable if baby is not...these are guidelines, not guarantees)

• Experiencing projectile vomiting and/or explosive diarrhea, which, it turns out, are not exaggerations after all

• Enjoying a good turn of peek-a-boo, or similar games

• Teething

• Discovering how high breast-feeding mom jumps when the new tooth starts working

• Finding *Jeffersons* reruns somewhat predictable

• Evincing jealousy of whatever Mom and Dad are having for dinner, which looks so much more interesting than whatever color mash baby is being served

• Using more than his fair share of the nation's landfills, thanks to "disposables"

• Developing an allergic reaction to either the peanut butter or the strawberries, and now you know why you were supposed to introduce them one at a time

WHAT YOUR WIFE MAY BE COMPLAINING ABOUT

- Exhaustion

- You

- Baby is already growing out of the cutest outfits

- That you actually tied the pacifier to the baby's outfit with a string

- How can you want to have sex, can't you see all the trouble it caused?

- How come you don't want to have sex, am I that unattractive?

- The state of children's television

- The nanny

- The absence of a nanny

- Everyone who meets your baby thinks she is a boy or he is a girl

- She was working really hard on a picture with crayons and then the baby scribbled on it

- She thought that the whole thing about your feet actually getting a half-size larger was just some kind of crazy legend made up to scare teenage girls into abstinence, but it has actually happened

- Wasted all that time listening to Mozart to increase the baby's intelligence before some other scientist proved it was a crock

THE ADVENT OF DADAISM

"Some books say that babies generally will say 'mama' first, others say 'dada.' I'm not saying I have a preference, I'll really be happy just to have a healthy, name-speaking baby. I'm just curious about it."

While some texts have claimed that "dada" or "papa" can come first, most experts agree that "mama" is the first name the baby will say. Yes, no matter how often you repeat "dada" in baby's ear while your wife is napping, the chances are that you will still have to be second in line for the ineffable thrill of being called by title.[5] Why is this? And is there any way around it?

Most mothers would be quick to point out that perhaps the fact that they did all the child-birthing, all of the breast-feeding, and most of the other parenting. ought to pay off in some dividend. There is a certain blunt validity to these claims; however, we would like to suggest another possibility.

This whole "mama" thing may be an etymological conspiracy whose roots lie as far back as the dawn of civilization. Hear us out. Babies' mouths and tongues have been basically the same since we gained the ability to use speech to communicate. The sound of "m" is easier to make, always has been. So babies always said "m" words first, and the mother, who happened to be around more because the males were off hunting, while they were tending the fire, decided to let the "m" sound be their name. Primitive man came back with some primitive possum on a sharp stick. "Say, what's the baby saying," he asks innocently. "Oh that? He's saying my name, mama. That's what he calls me." "Huh, that's interesting. Well, let me know when he comes up with a name for me, okay?"

So by all rights, fathers today, being equal and cooperative partners, should have the right to be called "mama" instead of "dada." That way they would have at least a fair shot of having the baby call their name first. Perhaps we could work out some sort of rotating schedule for the whole civilization? Since, for all of the second millennium, we used "m" sounds for mothers, so now fathers should get to take over for the next thousand years. It's only fair.

TEETHING PAIN

"Our little guy is having a miserable time with teething. We've tried cold teething rings, but once he gets too tired to gnaw, he just lies there crying. My mother says a little Scotch rubbed on the gums is just

---

5. One father objected to this statement, claiming that his baby said "dada" first and very early, too. However, upon further questioning, it became apparent that while the child was saying "dada" he was not actually referring to anything, or anyone in particular.

the thing, and that they all did it and we came out just fine. But is it really okay?"

It probably isn't going to do any harm unless you're pouring a shot glass down the baby, and the alcohol does have a mild numbing effect. Your basic over-the-counter medication for teething pain, like Anbesol, will probably work a whole lot better, but certainly isn't as much fun to administer. Baby's little face when the Scotch hits is a sight to behold. A drop or two on one finger is plenty. (Seriously, any more than that would be a big mistake; for a baby, a swig of hard liquor could be a deadly poison.)

After you've made the decision to use a little Scotch, the next question is obvious: which Scotch is best for my child's development? As the saying goes, you teach good taste by giving kids things that taste good. So domestic blended Scotches are out. You'll definitely want to go with a single malt from the bonny highlands of Scotland. Some new fathers swear by the Islay, and the lowlands have their proponents, too, but if you're getting started, there's no better place than Speyside. Following are just a few suggestions. They are pricey, of course, but you wouldn't want to scrimp on something as important as your baby. Besides, they also provide a handy self-medicating anesthetic to ease the pains you yourself suffer in the home and workplace. And don't forget to stock your home with the bottles you choose well in advance of teething, because you certainly don't want to face a teething crisis with nothing

but a bottle of Jack Daniels in the house!

1. **Tamnavulin**. Light in both color and body, it's still blessed with the complex earthy palate that makes single malts the glory that they are. The nose is sherry with some hint of barley, the palate is lemony and smooth, the finish oaky and aromatic.

2. **Cragganmore**. The aroma of this Speyside wonder is a festival, the body firm, the palate is delicate—perfect for delicate taste buds.

3. **Glenlivet**. The best known and most widely available, but don't hold its popularity against it. Its fame derives from its outstandingly clean, soft and flowery character, with a gentle, warming finish any teether will appreciate.

What You May Be Concerned About

STILL NOT SLEEPING?

"All right, this has gone just about far enough. We're going to have a serious sleep intervention in this house unless we start sleeping through the night. "

One frequent cause of continued sleep issues is working parents' syndrome. Here's what happens. You finally get home from work at 6:30 or

7:00. After a long day in the salt mines, you're ready to enjoy the fruits of your labor, some quality family time. You deserve baby smiles, baby gurgles. You should get to see baby's new trick. Let the parenting party begin! And baby's up for it. What could be more exciting than Dad, or Mom and Dad arriving? You might think this would be perfect, really wear that baby out with fun and then look forward to a long restful night. But it doesn't work that way. Baby will never learn the difference between day and night if evenings are always so great. Let's face it, babies are naturally the most fun in the morning. Especially the ones who are sleeping through the night. If you could do it, working eleven to seven would be ideal.

Does this mean you are doomed? No, it just means you have to be prepared to gear down earlier in the evening. Play and have fun after work, but starting a good hour before crib time you should stop with the baby-tossing and daddy-garoo games. Music should be of the soothing smooth jazz or string quartet variety. For most parents, being boring at night will come naturally. It's a by-product of exhaustion. But others will need to plan to be dull. And no matter what time of night, whether it's the evening, or during a late-night feeding, set your television on "stun." Watch an old Spencer Tracy movie instead of *Predator 4*. Watch *The Donna Reed Show* reruns instead of loud, garish *Third Rock from the Sun* reruns. And no *Springer*! How many times do we have to tell you?

What It's Important to Know
BABY LITERATURE

Though it is early to expect your baby to focus on even the simplest book for very long, the sooner you can get in the habit of reading together, the better. After all, reading *Pat the Bunny* three hundred times is fine, but if you can get in five or six hundred times, all the better. And what makes *Good Night Moon* a classic is that you're always finding something new in it. Either that, or reading any single book more than twice a day for a year can set off hallucinations.

You'll probably start with a few bored books—we mean board books, of course. These have the advantage of being tear-proof and the disadvantage of only having ten or fifteen pages. How can you deal with the inevitable tedium? We found that creating little challenges for yourself can make it easier. Try to memorize the text and read the whole book with your eyes closed. Perform in a Scottish accent, or like a favorite actor or personality. *The Hungry Caterpillar* sounds great as if read by Jimmy Stewart, and *Hop on Pop* as read by Richard Nixon can be riveting.

The biggest challenge are picture books. At least when a book offers some text, no matter how minimal, you can set your brain on a sort of autopilot. The pages flip, the words are uttered, the ritual is performed. (You'll find later on that your toddler has memorized his favorite books, and will not abide any ad-libs. Such changes may amuse him, but he will also insist that the actual text be maintained as well; yes, that will mean reading it again, possibly from the beginning.) But with a picture book, you're on your own. Each page requires you to interpret and create a sentence or question of some sort to bring closure to the experience. It may not seem like much now, but once you're actually in sleep-deprived, drool-covered full-fatherhood mode, just firing off enough synapses to say something like "there are some of the clowns in the circus" is pretty tough. And of course all the clever postmodern children's book illustrators don't make it easy: "This is a cow driving a car. That's silly. Okay, now the cow has to stop by the big, uh, jungle gym, to let these ducks...or geese... these birds cross...over to the, well, some sort of big bird party."

What books should you be reading? At this age it hardly matters. Read baby whatever book you're reading. (One friend made it a habit to read Shakespeare aloud to his kids; he figured it made about as much sense as anything else, and it would probably be easier to get a baby to listen to Shakespeare than to get a teenager to read it.) Eventually, you will want to move on to age-appropriate texts. Most likely, friends and relatives will stock your shelves for you. Then you'll purchase a few classics you remember from your own childhood. You'll soon have quite a little library. The average parent has fourteen different versions of an animal alphabet book, each with its own solution to the X problem, ranging from "X is in Fox" to "X isn't for anything" to "X is for xerxes" which is, apparently, some sub-genus of the cockatoo, although our dictionary says it's just a Greek king. The basic library will include a handful of Dr. Seuss; *Go Dog, Go;* some Sesame Street products (*The Monster At the End of This Book* is especially recommended). Also *Goodnight Moon, Harold and the Purple Crayon*, Richard Scarry's *Big Book of Things* (don't miss out on seeing the Pig Family sitting down to a big ham dinner!), and, of course, *Pat the Bunny.*

Pat the Bunny is the all-time number-one bestseller for babies.[6] If you don't know it, you will soon. It's a series of things for baby to feel or smell or look at. It's a classic, but it has changed over the years. A long time ago, to our best recollection, the page that suggested you "feel daddy's scratchy face" was produced in such a way that the entire natural beard area of the drawn face was covered with a sandpaper texture. Apparently, this was too expensive or complicated to continue producing, and more recent editions still suggest that you feel his scratchy face but now only a small kidney-shaped patch on Daddy's face is actually scratchy. One friend of ours would always amuse himself by reading the text on this page as "touch the strange mole on daddy's face." You could argue that he was offering a more realistic verbal appraisal of the situation.

---

6. This may be largely due to the fact that every baby chews, mauls, and otherwise goes through at least two or three copies.

What to Be Terrified About This Month

RARE DISEASES

It seems like only yesterday that your reading and anxiety was focused on all the potential birth disorders—cerebral palsy, pyloric stenosis, celiac disease, cleft palate, sickle cell anemia, spina bifida—but now it's time to move on. There are still plenty of terrible things that your baby can contract, develop or exhibit. We don't intend for this work to offer a complete discussion of all the possibilities. This is merely a place to begin.

First, there are the health hazards that face us all: mosquito-borne encephalitis, Lyme disease, rabies, bronchial pneumonia, tuberculosis, vampire bites, and implantation of outer-space aliens who will take over from inside while your outward appearance remains normal. There are also diseases and conditions that are more likely to occur in babies and children than adults: bronchiolitis, chicken pox, fifth disease, scarlet fever, herpangina, hand-foot-mouth disease, mumps, German measles and whooping cough.

There, you ought to be thoroughly petrified now. And yes, you can buy one of those "boy in the plastic bubble" setups if you want to. It's a little inconvenient, but what price can you put on peace of mind?

A FEW THINGS TO SAY TO LET HER KNOW THAT YOU ARE CARING, SENSITIVE AND UP ON THE REQUIRED READING

Oh come on, reading a little real information isn't so bad. You might learn something.

1. "Teething begins around now (although its onset can range anywhere from two to twelve months) with the eruption (ouch, that makes it sound really painful!) of two lower central incisors, then the two lateral incisors. There will be a total of twenty baby teeth. These first teeth allow the baby to make a new series of noises and sounds, and lead to more vocal experimentation."

2. "The most common allergic reactions in babies during the first year of life—and therefore, foods to be avoided entirely until later—are to dairy, wheat, eggs, and acidic fruits like strawberries, raspberries, citrus and tomatoes. A list that also offers more proof that tomatoes are a fruit, not a vegetable."

3. "Seven-month-olds have now mastered their own hands, and one of the most interesting thing to do—besides grabbing—is exploring textures. You'll find baby is stroking the rug, sofa, floor, your face, hair, sweaters—just trying out new sensations with a hands-on approach."

CHAPTER TEN

The Eighth, Ninth & Tenth Months

WHAT YOUR ABOVE-AVERAGE BABY MAY BE DOING

• Cruising: walking with furniture's aid

• Waving bye-bye (or hello, it's like shalom)

• Reacting to the word "no"—not obeying, just reacting

• Snaking forward on the belly

• Crawling

• Making you wonder, ever so briefly as he mashes rice cereal into his forehead, if maybe he's not so above average after all

• Saying a word or two besides mama and dada

• Standing alone briefly, or even for an extended period

• Playing catch—rolling a ball back and forth

• Drinking from a spout cup

• Taking a nasty fall out of the walker, after your wife said it was a bad idea to use it in the first place, but it was a gift from your sister and it looked like fun

• Somehow managing to leave sticky patches on every surface in the house including some that he couldn't possibly have reached

• Making people smile and go "Aww!" almost everywhere; and in direct inverse proportion, making everyone frown and go "Uhh!" as you look for your airline seats

WHAT YOUR WIFE MAY BE COMPLAINING ABOUT

• Exhaustion

• You

• Has become convinced that baby has attention deficit disorder

• Just when the baby is finally on a reasonable sleep schedule, wham!—the daylight-savings time adjustment comes along and confuses everything

• Visits to the park have revealed the sad truth that your baby's name, chosen for charm, nonconformity and originality—was also chosen by a full 30 percent of the other parents

• Her books about baby care and parenting are long and tedious and detailed and long, while yours conveniently puts three months together

• The nanny gets to spend all the fun time with baby and by the time your wife gets home it's nothing but cranky city

• Still can't believe they retired "pineapple" from five fruit Lifesavers

• That you don't believe in the "family bed"

• Having a baby has doubled your household monthly intake of catalogs and junk mail

• Rising mortgage rates

• That it's pathetic that getting a chance to read the newspaper in peace for a half-hour should feel so luxurious

What You May Be Concerned About

DROOLING

"All of a sudden my little bundle of joy has turned into a human spigot. He's throwing saliva like a little St. Bernard. I can't quite believe this is normal."

The period of teething can lead to seemingly endless drooling. This is a period where suddenly it doesn't seem all that surprising that the human body is about 60 percent water. Is there something cute about the thin string of spittle hanging constantly from baby's chin? Maybe for the first week, but not the second, third or fourth. The cloths and bibs that were once available for spit-up are now in constant use again, to stem the tide. Taking photographs becomes a new challenge, as the shiny chin becomes an issue. The open-mouthed stare that once bespoke a newcomer's curiosity and hunger for knowledge becomes, with the addition of drool, frankly, a little dopey looking. Like a snail, your baby will now leave a trail as he pulls himself across the kitchen floor. The front of every shirt is not just moist, but soaked through.

How much drool is too much? Look for signs of dehydration: hollow eyes, infrequent or unusually dark urination, dry skin. How long is too long for the drooling to go on? After the first four teeth have erupted, most of the teething-related drooling should subside. If not, drooling will still diminish and most likely end when solid foods are being eaten regularly. Excessive drooling will not be seen again until the advent of puberty.

What You May Be Concerned About

CIRCLEHEAD

"This may sound strange, but I seem to have developed a circular red mark on my forehead. My wife just keeps laughing at me. What's happening to me?"

You're suffering from one of the most common—but fortunately, eminently curable—afflictions of early fatherhood. Circlehead is caused when fathers seek to amuse their children by attaching toys that are meant to be stuck onto high-chairs or cribs onto their foreheads. This generally succeeds in making baby giggle; but it can easily lead to a round "hickey" that can last for up to a week, depending on how long the suction cup remained in place. This generally succeeds in making Mommy giggle.

NOT ENOUGH INFORMATION

"Hey, I'm reading along, month-by-month, following all the developmental details and changes and all of a sudden, wham—you're lumping the eighth, ninth and tenth months together? What's that about?"

Oh yeah, like you were really paying that much attention. Think of it as one of those "Special" issues of a magazine that covers two weeks. Okay, if it's so important, tell me in which month is it typical for a baby to first follow an object moving in an arc 12–16 inches from his face? When can you expect the two lower teeth? What are the first foods to try, and when?

Eight, nine, ten, what's the big deal? Most babies' development falls within a broad normal range. Oh, all right, the truth is when we wrote up all the notes on important events we got mixed up and couldn't figure out which was which, so we figured, what the heck, it's all in the same basic area. We're just here to help you make it through the year intact. If you're looking for specific information, there are tons of tedious tomes out there with minute-by-minute charts. Another advantage of lumping these months together is that now chapter 11 is about eleven-month-olds, and chapter 12 is about bankruptcy—I mean twelve-month-olds. (Although twelve-month-olds *can* be related to bankruptcy; have you checked your monthly budget lately?)

Anyway, haven't you got better things to do than to tell me What You May Be So Darned Concerned About? Go take a nap, or write up some cute stories for the baby book. You're too tired to chronicle every "first" in the baby book, aren't you? Why not write your very own chapter about the subtle but important distinctions between an eight-month-old and a ten-month-old, then glue it in this book and write your name on the cover. Go for it, we've learned that sharing is nice.

MAKING BABY LAUGH

As the dad there are very few areas of child care or child development in which you can take the lead, or provide any expertise that your wife has not already mastered. However, there are a couple of subjects in which men traditionally prove superior to women. One is teaching toddler boys how to pee standing up. Another is making baby laugh.

Most theorists believe that this is not an innate skill, so much as an adaptive one. In other words, men aren't good for much else, so they might as well be willing to wear underpants on their head, walk like an elephant, or talk like Donald Duck if it gets a laugh. Women seem less able to release their inhibitions in these contexts. Either it's related to self-esteem issues in young adulthood or they're just too damn tired. Another possibility is that when Mom—the foodgiver and center of the universe—appears to be losing touch with reality, it's too threatening to the baby. They will just get worried. On the other hand, what if Dad, the man who comes when the windows turn black, were to go off the deep end? Well, he'd be missed but there are lots of other people who could fill his role.

But do babies even know what's cuckoo goofy and what's not? Certainly, and the proof is that if they didn't, they wouldn't be laughing. Without getting into too much detail (see Sigmund Freud's *Jokes and Their Relation to the Subconscious* or Henri Bergson's *On Laughter* for more analysis), humor results from leaps of consciousness, connections that are made in our mind that shortcut our expectations.

That's why babies don't laugh for a while. They have no expectations. They have barely moved from the state of "I am the universe" to the "I seem to be a separate being" and are a long way from the "If there is a heaven, what makes people there behave themselves?" However, by the eighth month of life, there are enough expectations and enough knowledge that laughs become a regular possibility. For example, your basic peek-a-boo goes a little something like this, from a cognitive point of view: "That's Dad's face— wait, now there are just those hands, I guess he's gone now....hey! He's back!" Basically, baby has an expectation that people will come and go—but not so quickly!

Your challenge as a father is to find our what makes your baby laugh loudest and hardest. For those seeking assistance, there is an entire guidebook available on the subject, *97 Ways to Make a Baby Laugh* (Workman Publishing, 1997). The authors guarantee success, but frankly, we question their methodology. It is our theory that no two babies are alike and that it is, in fact, very difficult to predict what will make a baby laugh. Sadly, from personal experience we know that a sure-fire comedy bit for one baby can make another baby burst into horrified wailing.

Moreover, making a baby laugh should not be a matter of following someone else's formula, but an improvisational experiment. Getting there is half the fun. The only thing predictable about a baby's laughing is that it will be unpredictable. You'll no doubt end up yelling "Honey, get in here—I've discovered the funniest thing in the world" and demonstrate tilting your head forward until your baseball cap falls off. Even more mundane events can sometimes cause peals of infant laughter. And the second ten times you do it are even funnier than the first ten times. One day picking up a stray half grape between your finger and thumb will seem hysterical. The next day, you can reenact John Cleese's entire "Ministry of Silly Walks" sketch and get only a confused, perhaps even concerned, stare. Our advice is just to keep trying, use whatever material works over and over. Think *Three Stooges*, not Noël Coward. No in-law jokes, or blue humor. Slapstick is king! And never tell the assembled friends and relatives "this always works." That'll be the day it will cease to be amusing.

All your efforts will be rewarded because you'll eventually get the laugh, and nothing could be sweeter. And get those laughs while you can, Dad! Infants will lap up the easy physical comedy; preschoolers will enjoy that, along with the goofiest puns, riddles and knock-knock jokes; but eventually you will find yourself trying to get a laugh out of a dour ten-year-old who would rather be playing computer games. Tilting forward until your hat falls off isn't going to cut it anymore.

What to Be Terrified About This Month

IT'S DEFINITELY YOUR TURN

By now the familiar wrinkled nose, and then the call of "It's your turn" have become a routine. But things are about to take a turn for the uglier. Perhaps the reaction is not terror so much as a truly profound disgust, but with the introduction of new foods comes a whole new world of diaper changes, indigestion, and interesting noises. For this month, we'll simply provide the top ten words you'd rather not hear, read, think about or face:

10. Crusty

9. Yellowish

8. Seedy

7. Acrid

6. Loose

5. Patrilineal

4. Obstructed

3. Explosive

2. Fungal

1. Inconsolable

A FEW THINGS TO SAY TO LET HER KNOW THAT YOU ARE CARING, SENSITIVE AND UP ON THE REQUIRED READING

You should appreciate that, while these sections may not be as funny as some of the others, they took a lot more research. That should count for something.

1. "Studies have shown a correlation between children's intelligence and how many words they heard as an infant and toddler, so it's important to maintain a dialogue even before there is any real comprehension."

2. "Instead of moving all our books from reachable shelves, one source suggests that we could just pack them in tightly enough so that the baby can't pull them out."

3. "The trick to leaving your baby alone with a sitter, without a crisis, is nonchalance. Have the sitter arrive with plenty of time before you actually have to leave, so the baby can adjust to the new presence. Then make the departure short and sweet. One kiss ought to do it. Long explanations of why Mommy has to leave and how long she'll be gone and why she's wearing perfume are only likely to increase the anxiety. Both yours and baby's."

CHAPTER ELEVEN

The Eleventh Month

WHAT YOUR ABOVE-AVERAGE BABY MAY BE DOING

- Pointing to objects of desire

- Using "Mama" and "Dada" to refer to each individual parent

- Using words (that only he knows the meaning of)

- Walking with a helping hand

- Insisting on walking with a helping hand and thus causing you severe back strain

- Cooperating with getting dressed—putting a hand out for the shirt to go on

- Resisting getting dressed—pulling the hand you need away

- Being your willing puppet as you re-create the ballet *Swan Lake* with baby as prima ballerina (equally willing to do the Peppermint Twist or to shake it up to some Western swing—Bob Wills and the Texas Playboys' "Stay a Little Longer" works particularly well)

- Experiencing separation anxiety

- Getting his teeth brushed, all four of them

- Becoming seriously addicted to an automatic swinging chair

- Eating as much as 15 to 20 percent of the food placed in front of him (leaving 80 to 85 percent to be worked into every available crevice in the high chair and used as facial cream, hair conditioner and projectiles)

- Moving on to a second photo album, having filled the first with photos

WHAT YOUR WIFE MAY BE COMPLAINING ABOUT

• Exhaustion

• You

• Men in general, with you as simply a classic example

• Has become convinced that the baby is an introvert

• That annoying columnists, educational specialists, and self-righteous friends have made her feel so guilty about using the TV as a baby-sitter now and then

• Losing train of thought

• Hating to admit it, but that she has become a regular reader of the "Baby Blues" comic strip

• The fact that you are only likely to give her a back massage if you can also watch a baseball game on TV

• Furthermore, the fact that she loves a massage so much that she now knows the difference between a squeeze bunt and a safety squeeze

• Either they're making crossword puzzles harder, or her intelligence level is actually slipping—don't answer that!

• Doesn't buy the argument that the family budget doesn't need a line for entertainment because the baby is your entertainment

• Find-a-word is also too hard

LOOK WHO'S TALKING

"My daughter is finally getting the idea of talking. Should we be trying to teach her specific words? Is there anything we can do to encourage her?"

As we have mentioned elsewhere, it is vital to maintain a dialogue with your infant. When the words start to come, you may feel the desire to take a more pedantic approach, but it really isn't necessary. Your baby wants to talk! She'll pick up the words she needs, because she's probably in almost as much a hurry as you. After all, ten months of stories, complaints, ideas—there's a backlog to communicate.

Which words can you expect to hear? After mama and dada (or papa, if you've been speaking French to your infant, as you should have been in order to help him get into an Advanced Placement high school French class, and thus, into the college of his choice), baby's first words are naturally words that are especially important or functional in his limited world.

TEN COMMON EARLY WORDS

1. Juice

2. Up

3. Bottle

4. Binky (pacifier)

5. Eyes (and Nose and Mouth—the face parts that baby has been staring at so much)

6. Cookie

7. Ball

8. Gimme

9. Bye-bye

10. Mine

WORDS THAT BABY DOES NOT CONSIDER SO IMPORTANT AND CAN BE LEARNED LATER

1. No

2. Clean

3. Stop

4. Nap

5. Please

6. Scholarship

7. Share

8. Sympathy

9. Tired

10. Really Tired

MOMMY'S TURN

"I know, I know. She's been with the baby all day. I've been—according to her—hanging out with friends and having coffee and talking about sports and TV all day. Still, isn't there ever a time when I can ask for a break from active baby duty?"

Oh, sure. Why didn't you ask us earlier? There are plenty of reasonable and necessary excuses that you can offer your wife, and that she will naturally accept. Here are seven perfectly adequate reasons for not taking the helm:

1. You're literally holding up the ceiling.

2. Letting go of the steering wheel probably isn't such a great idea.

3. You're not actually there; and are more than two hours' travel time from home.

4. You're juggling fireballs, and if you drop them, they will cause the house to burn down.

5. You're on the phone settling a diplomatic crisis between nations of no fewer than one million people.

6. It's three-all in the bottom of the ninth. (Just kidding.)

7. If you stand up and cross the room, the bad guys outside will open fire again.

DRESSING FOR BABY SUCCESS

"If I get sent back to choose a different T-shirt one more time, I'm going to lose it. Why is my wife so obsessed about what the baby is wearing? It's going to be covered in drool, apple juice and rice paste within two hours anyway."

Men are capable of changing diapers. They can feed a baby a bowl of mashed whatever. They can probably even manage an evening alone so that Mommy can go to a friend's wedding shower. But there is no doubt that they cannot, or will not, master the ability to mix and match a baby's wardrobe.

Mothers care about what the baby looks like because they are transferring their own frustrated fashion desires. Maybe they can't manage much beyond a gray sweatshirt and jeans, but that baby needs to wear the black stretch pants that match the sunflower shirt and the yellow booties. Babies can go through three and four outfits a day, what with spills, meals and accidents.

The end result is that there are dozen of outfits to choose from, making Dad's job darn near impossible. The only hope is to memorize a few combinations and be prepared to lie. "You always put her in the lion jumper." "Uh, yeah, I guess I just really think it's cute."

What You May Be Concerned About

CALLING THE PEDIATRICIAN

"Why should I have to call the pediatrician just because my wife is too embarrassed to call anymore? It's her paranoid question, not mine, and besides, we both know that I won't ask it 'right' and we'll be left with an unsatisfying, incomplete answer."

Because she asked you to. Anyway, what are the odds you're going to have to do anything but leave a message with the receptionist? Then, later, whoever forgets and picks up the phone gets to do the honors.

What It's Important to Know

FATHER'S HEALTH ISSUES

There are many thorough guides to potential health issues for the baby. (If you're looking here for advice on high fever or a persistent cough, you're in real trouble, mister.) For women's health, especially regarding breast-feeding, and other mothering issues, there are no end of magazines, Web sites and guides. But the special issues relating to being an active father are often over-

looked. Fortunately for you, we are righting this wrong. Here is a handy index of first aid and long-term health issues, just for fathers.

Circlehead

A cold compress can help minimize the long-term effect (see page 104 for a full discussion).

Colleague flu seclusion

This is the side effect of having a cold or flu but going to work anyway because you're not going to get any rest at home with the wife and baby. The result is annoyed coworkers who try to avoid sitting next to you in meetings because they don't want to catch it.

Groucho syndrome

Helping cruising toddlers by holding their hands can be hazardous to the lower back. The same can be said for pushing tricycles and other vehicles. Last but not least, tall men should seriously consider buying a stroller handle extender (available in many children's specialty shops) that will allow you to walk the baby without leaning forward the entire time.

Hyperextended nostril

Babies loves exploring the faces that they have spent so long studying visually. Poking and prodding is natural, but don't be afraid to say "Yeow!" when pain is inflicted. Just be aware that a baby may not see that as a cry of distress so much as just another interesting phenomenon to explore.

Lapular trauma

Blunt trauma to the lap, so to speak, caused by jumping or running toddlers. Just take a few minutes and try to breathe.

Matrimonial Affective Disorder

The general term for a large number of mental health issues related to your failings as a human being and partner. Better known by its acronym, MAD, or colloquially as "being in the doghouse." Cures includes abject apologies, flowers, and back rubs.

Sleep deprivation

The only known cure is a business trip, with no early morning meetings and a duration of at least three days.

Sooo big backache

When playing "how big is baby," remember that throwing your arms upward can be just as dramatically effective as leaning your body backwards, with much less strain on the spinal column.

What to Be Terrified About This Month

UNSAFE AT ANY SPEED

Ever thought about all the new ways your baby will be able to get hurt once he is able to get all around the house? Sure you have. But perhaps we can help you come up with a few possibilities you haven't considered. Here are some safety tips, starting with the basics:

• No balloons in the house. Pieces of them can be easily inhaled and can't be seen in X-rays.

• Install a smoke detector if you haven't already. Babies are more susceptible to smoke inhalation than adults.

• Don't leave baby alone in a room with pets, young siblings, or kidnappers.

• Leaving a baby alone in a room with a grandparent should be done with discretion; you may find that your six-month-old has gotten his first ice-cream cone while you were away.

• Don't leave your baby in the car while shopping without rolling the window down a little so he can get some air...Kidding! Just kidding! Of course, you should never leave the baby in the car at all.

• Don't practice shooting apples off your baby's head. Children under the age of five cannot be depended upon to stand perfectly still.

• Don't let babies cut their own hair. They always mess up the back.

• Don't leave your wife alone with baby for more than forty-eight hours, business trip or no business trip. This is more for your personal safety than baby's.

A FEW THINGS TO SAY TO LET HER KNOW THAT YOU ARE CARING, SENSITIVE AND UP ON THE REQUIRED READING

Don't skip this section. You will be surprised how impressed people are when you actually spout some relevant piece of information about babies and development.

1. "Don't forget that part of your eleventh-month-old's experiments and observations have to do with you. You're being studied. So, while you're wondering how many times can dropping the spoon off the high chair be of any interest, your baby is probably wondering how many times will Dada pick up the spoon and put it back on my tray?

2. "When babies are just learning to talk, you have to be prepared to learn their words as much as they learn yours. If your baby creates a word 'gah-boo' and uses it to ask to be picked up, you shouldn't try to correct them, or replace it with 'up.' It's better not to frustrate their attempts to communicate at this point. Take up the use of 'gah-boo' yourself for now, and there will be plenty of time to correct baby later."

3. "They say that you shouldn't appear to be disgusted or displeased while you're changing a diaper. You don't want to give them the idea that what they've done is wrong, and it's never too soon to start preparing for that psychological watershed that is toilet training."

CHAPTER TWELVE

The Twelfth Month

WHAT YOUR ABOVE-AVERAGE BABY MAY BE DOING

• Walking

• Or crawling, but really quite exceptionally fast

• But, not quite as much as your brother's ten-month-old is doing, which is extremely irritating

• Babbling

• Responding to physical gestures—look there, take this

• Executing bowel movements that require as many as six or even eight wipes

• Taking a full frontal dive into his first birthday cake

• Refusing to allow a hat to remain on

• Using a few proper nouns (it's usually around the age of ten or eleven years that you'll hear the use of improper nouns)

• Finding the seams in your childproofing (it's like finding the seams in a zone defense, got it?)

• Gaining the ability to distinguish between food and the soil in potted houseplants, but not caring

• Gaining the ability to distinguish between Lenny and Squiggy

• While randomly typing on the computer keyboard, somehow irreversibly changing the settings so the screen saver comes on after three seconds of inactivity

• Finding wads of wrapping paper far more interesting (and tastier, too!) than any toy yet invented

WHAT YOUR WIFE MAY BE COMPLAINING ABOUT

- Exhaustion

- You

- The charm of baby's newfound mobility has quickly become a nightmare, as the house must now be completely childproofed again

- That the baby clearly chose you over her at some moment, even if it was a rare event

- The remote control has become baby's favorite teether, which means you can't get too attached to watching a particular channel

- Has become convinced that the baby is left-handed, and a lifetime of awkward handwriting, bumping elbows at dinner, and using uncomfortable scissors looms ahead

- Any truly responsible father would have taken an infant CPR class by now

- No one else seems to recognize the clear outlines of a face that baby has drawn with a "burnt sienna" crayon

- Women like dancing more than men, women are better at dancing then men, so how exactly did men get the job of "leading?"

- Can't believe you would want to cut your baby boy's adorable ringlets of hair just because of a few stray playground comments

- Crayons are not a "nontraditional" food—you shouldn't have let the baby chew them

THINGS YOU CAN AND CANNOT ACCOMPLISH WHILE LYING ON A RUG WITH THE BABY AFTER YET ANOTHER SLEEPLESS NIGHT

Can't...take a nap, or the baby will somehow manage to roll over and get a foot jammed in the iron grillwork side table.

Can...rest your eyes. "I saw...it's okay. I got it."

Can't...balance a checkbook because it requires more intellectual capacity than is available and besides the pen and calculator are irresistible.

Can...carefully comb all the rug fringe to fall in the same direction.

Can't...clean the house.

Can...dust the tops of the books on the bottom shelf with your thumb.

Can't...have a cup of coffee. (Too dangerous!)

Can...roll the top of your sock neatly all the way down as far as it will go on your ankle, then roll it back up to the top.

Can't...read the newspaper unless you don't mind the shredding that will happen simultaneously (which, by the way, is a great game, so long as you can get past the eating-the-paper problem, and don't mind the ink rubbing off onto everything).

Can...adjust your watchband to its widest setting and wear it on your forearm, then take it off and set it at its narrowest and try to imagine someone with a wrist that small.

Can't...remember how you ended up in your job.

Can...assess your body and make plans to work out.

Can't...do stomach crunches and "baby-ups"—the spirit is willing, but the flesh is weak.

Can...click your pen out and in repeatedly, trying to establish by analysis of the sound alone exactly how the retractable feature works.

Can't...remember what you were supposed to do this afternoon. It wasn't groceries, or laundry. Oh, well.	**Can**...scout your available epidermis for issues: ear or nostril hair, uneven cuticles or sideburns, spots missed shaving, areas of immediate or potential hair loss.
Can't...get any real work or reading done.	**Can**...flip through women's magazines looking at models.
Can't...teach an eleven-month-old baby to play double solitaire.	**Can**...listen to music. Hey, it's something, right?

What You May Be Concerned About

BOREDOM

"I think I'm a pretty devoted Dad, been reading up, mastered all the basic skills, but when I'm on duty there are times when I feel like I'm about to lose my mind. I love my baby, but he's boring!"

Often, watching the baby is just that: watching. You sit, you stare. You've demonstrated all the possible uses of each toy. You've talked at length to the baby, explaining what all the items in the room are, and who chose them. You briefly attempted to hypnotize the baby, and then realized: what would you do if it worked? You can't put the television on without feeling guilty, unless there's a ball game on because that's okay— besides, most daytime television is only slightly less tedious than watching an infant gum a rubber fire truck.

We don't really have an answer for the boredom, but you shouldn't feel guilty. It's natural to be bored by watching another person drool on the same toy for fifteen months. You shouldn't be trying to do anything but survive these periods. Guilt over not accomplishing anything has no place in the on duty father. Here's a list that might offer some solace.

What You May Be Concerned About

OCCUPATIONAL TRAINING

"I am a blacksmith by trade. My father was a blacksmith, as was his father before him. The McGregor clan has always been smithies. Now my wife is telling me that she thinks that a wee set of bellows isn't an appropriate toy for my son. What do I do?"

While there is no evidence that choice of toys will have an impact on your offspring's future career choice (well, of course there's no evidence, what sort of cockamamie scientist would actually invest time and effort to establish that?), it certainly couldn't hurt to expose the boy to the tools of his future trade. Bellows seems like a nice choice, compared to hammer and tongs.

It's not unusual to give children, even infants, toys that reflect potential occupations and professions. Interestingly, if you look at the most popular of such toys—farms and farm animals, dump trucks and construction sites, building blocks, fireman and policeman outfits, little lawnmowers—you might surmise that, basically, we encourage our offspring to take up blue collar occupations. Then again, perhaps we are just trying to get it out of their systems. More likely, the "Wee Corporate Lawyer," "Little Regional Office Manager" and "My First Advertising Portfolio" kits just didn't sell as well. Everybody does have a little doctor's kit, too—so there are some very young professionals out there. Why do we choose the blue collar toys? Wouldn't we all rather be building a house than arranging financing? Arresting criminals rather than managing portfolios? It's wish fulfillment, pure and simple.

THE BABY BOOK

"We started a baby book that first week, and we've written little notes on scraps of paper now and then, but we just haven't gotten organized enough to get it done. Should we be worried?"

Putting together a decent baby book is important, but there are some advantages to doing one that is incomplete, a bit slapdash, and done months or years after the actual events have taken place. Most importantly, you have not established a precedent that will be hard to match. When your second child (or third) wants to plead his case as having been neglected and underappreciated, the comparison of baby albums can be hard, incontrovertible evidence that you were more excited about and more devoted to the first-born. If you maintain an evenhanded neglect throughout all the baby books, you will never face this trauma.

That said, you should create some sort of baby book. Every moment may seem unforgettable now, but over the years the facts that "choppy" was the word for helicopter, and that Aunt Mildred's gift was the silver spoon, and that you went on your first family plane trip for Christmas will only live on if they are duly noted. Don't worry that you're not creating great literature. If you've been writing down little observations about the baby on scraps of paper, don't collect them, intending to transcribe them some-day. Just glue them in as they are. Your description of the first birthday party will have even more resonance written on the back of a Citibank envelope.

HOW TO THROW A FIRST BIRTHDAY PARTY

First of all, keep the guest list down to three. You, your wife and the baby. That's plenty. Even better, hire a baby-sitter and go out without the birthday baby. It's probably been a while.

Not festive enough? Okay, but don't say we didn't warn you. On the whole, one-year-olds hate parties—even if they are the guest of honor. There is a lot of noise, a sea of faces, and a high level of anxiety in Mom. They give you shiny crunchy paper, but won't let you eat it! Then they set the cake on fire, but won't let you see what fire feels like. Then everyone tries to get you to blow, and they don't seem to like it when you spit all over the cake trying. Here's the worst part: somebody brought other babies! Other babies are the worst. They don't make good faces or carry you, they play with your things, and they give you the unpleasant feeling that maybe you're not quite as unique

a creation as you once believed. Wait a second, that isn't even the worst part—the truly worst part of birth-days is that somebody puts a hat on you (pretty bad already) that has a tight elastic string that snaps against your face! Yeow!

On the positive side, it's really easy to throw a surprise party for a one-year-old. And the men can all gather around the barbecue and complain about their wives, while the women mill around the kitchen, complaining about their husbands. So all the adults will have a good time. Basically, if you are intent on throwing a first birthday party, go for it. Just remember that it's not really for the baby. Having the cute photo of the baby wailing uncontrollably in front of a cake that he wasn't even allowed to taste may be something you will one day treasure, but we're not so sure.

CONTAMINANTS!

We live a world of chemical addi-tives, a diminishing ozone layer, dioxins in our rainwater, and asbestos in our play sand. That's right, if you buy sand, even the stuff that is specifically made for chil-dren's sandboxes, it may contain chemical asbestos that can cause serious illness. Try pouring some sand yourself. If it raises dust, it may present a risk.

What else can you do? Quit smoking if you haven't already. And don't be afraid to be unpopular and insist on no smoking at all in your house or around the baby. There's enough nasty stuff in the air without adding recreational toxins. Check your house to make sure carbon monoxide buildup is not a problem. Don't burn newspaper—it has lead in it! Filter your water! Wash your fruits and vegetables! Get a microfilter vacuum cleaner right away!! Put this book down and wash your hands right away—don't you know that many printed materials contain trace elements of lead!!!

A FEW THINGS TO SAY IF SHE STILL DOESN'T GET IT TO LET HER KNOW THAT YOU ARE CARING, SENSITIVE AND UP ON THE REQUIRED READING

Listen, we all know that this isn't the fun part of the book, but do your homework! Jeepers, it's barely one page.

1. "It's very rare, but sometimes babies get very swollen cheeks in the summertime, due to something called "popsicle panniculitis" that they get from sucking on frozen popsicles, which can damage the tissues in the mouth. I guess that's sort of like the baby version of Slurpee brain-freeze?"

2. "Listen to this, honey: Infant massage has gained in popularity since being reintroduced from folk traditions in the 1970s—when else?—and can improve infants' vitality and responsiveness. But here's the best part...one of the scientists who has done work in this field, and wrote a paper studying tactile effects on preterm neonates, is Dr. Tiffany Field of the Touch Research Institute at the University of Miami. It's true. Now, if you got an e-mail from Dr. Tiffany of the Touch Research Institute, well, what would you think?"

3. "Sure, you get pre-boarding when you take an airplane trip, but did you know that strollers don't count as carry-on luggage? And that many airlines have special meals for babies and toddlers that you can order in advance? And if you travel first class on some international flights you can get a special baby amenity kit with diapers, bibs and a baby spoon?"

CHAPTER THIRTEEN

The Toddler Years

WHAT YOUR ABOVE-AVERAGE TODDLER MAY BE DOING

• Getting toilet trained (yes, someday the diapers will end)

• Talking in detail, picking up new vocabulary quickly, especially words that make grownups stare at them

• Recalling events from the distant past—weeks, even months earlier

• Predicting consequences, but ignoring that knowledge anyway

• Taste-testing practically everything

• Sharing (but don't count on it)

• Showing an awareness that Grandma is a pushover when it comes to sweets

• Picking up (despite all your efforts to censor television, movies, books, relatives, playmates) the first available longish object and pretending it is a gun

• Showing a healthy respect for big kids on bicycles

• Staring at people who look different in any way

• Creating mass quantities of abstract art, well beyond the needs of any refrigerator

• Drawing some representational art

• Trying out a little home hair-cutting on themselves

• Learning that jumping in Daddy's lap can really hurt Daddy if he doesn't know someone is about to jump in his lap

• Demanding a pet of his own

• First attempts at lying and deception, usually fairly transparent except for some especially gifted children who are bound for public office

WHAT YOUR WIFE MAY BE COMPLAINING ABOUT

• Exhaustion

• You

• That girls are supposed to be easier to toilet train

• Blue's clues are sometimes too hard to figure out

• Maybe if they didn't make "big kid" pull-up diapers, you wouldn't still be changing them

• That you threw out her handmade "toys" because they looked like oatmeal boxes to you

• Trying to edit kids' books for political correctness while in the midst of reading them aloud is too difficult

• Has become convinced the baby's cowlick will never go away, and sure it's cute now, but it'll look goofy in the senior class photo

• That balloons are incredibly dangerous and should be outlawed (and while we're at it let's just make a blanket law that would prevent clowns from scaring the bejeezus out of innocent toddlers)

• Someone sneaked into all the books she loved when she was growing up, and filled them full of sexism, racism, stereotyping and random violence

• No one else can understand your two-year-old's perfectly clearly stated sentences

• Misses having a little baby (uh oh...)

ESPN AS EDU-TAINMENT

"The Betsy says I watch too much sports on TV in front of junior. I say it's better than the crap she has on while she's on duty."

Watching sports on television is not only every man's God-given right, but a vital psychological need. Without a frequent infusion of play-by-play and color commentary, a man can wither away, cut off from the healing, life-affirming emotional excitement of sports. Sports provides the modern male with a rich emotional life. But don't try to convince her of this! Women seem to think that a rich emotional life is defined by relationships and expressive conversation; not by a deep and abiding loyalty to the Michigan State football team, or a meaningful relationship with *Baseball Tonight*.

So how can you defend the amount of televised sports you feel is appropriate? It's simple. You can never give your kids too much education. They should have a rich panorama of experience and learning. Television sports is a perfect vehicle for teaching. For one thing it is repetitive—the batter stands in each time, the football team lines up—which allows the child to practice cognitive skills. Repetition is a proven tool of preschool education, as anyone who has ever watched *Blue's Clues* can attest. As a series of visual images, most sports can be fairly easy to understand. As the child grows, deeper levels can be introduced.

Television sports are also safe and wholesome, as long as you steer clear of Foxy Boxing and Pro Wrestling. For the most part, athletes behave within a tightly circumscribed set of rules. They comport themselves with dignity (if you don't count obsessive spitting and the occasional temper tantrum) and while there is a certain amount of violence inherent in the games, there is just as much violence on daytime soap operas and in your average play school sandbox.

So how can you turn TV sports into edu-tainment? It's simple. Engage your child in a series of questions about the game. Make sure you keep it geared to their understanding. Remember, it will take time before you can just ask, "Do you think Clemens is through?" or "Should I take the Vikings at home plus six against the Packers?" But with frequent conversation, you'll be surprised how quickly your child can learn the basics of all your favorite sports. Best of all, you're not only teaching, you're sharing your time and bonding, too. Here are some simple examples to get you started.

COLORS

"Can you point to the boxer wearing the blue shorts?"

LEARNING BODY PARTS

"And what is the defensive back clutching? That's right, his knee!"

LETTERS

"What letters are on his cap? No, not a W, that's a good try, though. It's an interlocking N and Y."

BASIC MATH

"Uh oh! He swung and missed. Now how many strikes does McGwire have on him? How many strikes are left before he strikes out?"

TIME

"The basketball game has thirty-eight seconds left in the fourth quarter, which means with time-outs, commercials and stalling, there are about ten minutes left. Understand?"

SHARING

"Don't shoot it...Oh, you lousy...He should have passed the ball, and given his teammates a chance to shoot the ball."

SOCIAL SKILLS

"Bad defensive lineman, bad! He shouldn't have jumped on the quarterback after he had already thrown the ball. That's 'roughing the passer' and now his team is going to have a punishment."

CONSEQUENCES

"See, LeDoux is going to have to have a 'time-out' in the penalty box, because he was hitting with his stick."

CAREER PLANNING

"Yes, he throws the ball very hard. That's why he is getting 5.5 million dollars this year."

What You May Be Concerned About

IS MY SISTER'S KID GIFTED?

"Maybe my kid is no Einstein, but he's bright and curious, and he's gotten over the whole obsession with flushing things...anyway, the point is, my sister's son is the same age and, frankly, way ahead developmentally. Is there anything I can do to hold her kid back, I mean, help my kid out?"

Approaching your child's development from a competitive point of view will lead to inevitable disappointment. Each child has a unique timetable. Give your child a rich environment full of learning opportunities. Read to them, talk to them. But after that, let them learn at their own speed. Kids have a natural desire to master new skills and acquire new knowledge. Pressing that desire can set up negative associations that can hamper learning. Anyway, gifted is a very subjective word and your sister's boy is probably a real brat, and eventually your son will probably be able to beat him up. (And if it comes down to it, you can take your overachieving nephew aside and assure him that he is adopted, but that it's a secret and not to tell.)

What You May Be Concerned About

TAKING THE LORD'S NAME IN VAIN

"I've been known to use a little salty language now and then, and the wife is all over me to stop cursing in front of the baby. But it's a da...darn hard habit to break!"

That's why your mother told you not to swear in the first place; once it's a habit, you never know when you're going to suddenly let a zesty phrase slip out. Not that we have anything against using a few swear words, but their use should be strategic, for maximum impact.

In the meantime, the only answer is the R&E system: Repetition and Euphemism. You can't go cold turkey. You need to replace the offending vocabulary with more acceptable words and phrases. Then use the m frequently. Practice makes perfect. Here is a list of useful euphemisms for you to choose from. They are presented with exclamation marks to reflect their general usage.

1. Darn!

2. H E double hockey sticks!

3. Fudge!

4. Shi-ite! (Muslims)

5. Shucks!

6. Gee-willikers!

7. Jiminy Cricket!

8. My fat Aunt Harriet!

9. Cripes!

10. Fire truck!

Are you going to sound ridiculous saying these phrases? Heck, yes! Oops, how did we forget that one...

11. Heck

Naturally you are going to sound ridiculous, and after you say these phrases often enough you will find your urge to curse withering away entirely.

| What You May Be Concerned About | What It's Important to Know |

PICK ME A WINNER

TODDLER TELEVISION

"All right, this is a little embarrassing, but I know my kid isn't the first one to do it. He's two, barely mastered using his hands and barely figured out where own his face is...and practically the first thing he does is pick a booger and try to eat it! What the heck is that about?"

For decades, scientists have debated the issue. Is it nature or nurture that is the predominant force in forming human character? To what degree does our genetic predisposition drive us? How much impact does our environment have on our intelligence? Our moral character? Our desire to taste things that come out of our nose? Could this behavior, repulsive to most adults, be in some way naturally selected in the evolutionary process? Do we have any answers? Will mankind ever have answers? Or will we just keep posing questions? Will we be able to get to the end of this paragraph without using a period? We think not.

After the first year, the lure of television will prove too strong for all but the most radical parents. The question is how much television, and which shows. How much is a simple matter. As little as possible. Which shows is a more difficult issue. There are more and more options every day. However, we would like to offer one general guideline. We believe that television functions as a teaching tool best when the show is of interest to adults. In other words, you're a better judge of what is good for your kids than you may think. You should like it.

Our belief that television should not "talk down" to kids, or pander to their level of comprehension is not without controversy. There are different schools of thought on this matter. The details and arguments could, and actually have, filled numerous books. Should the show be repetitive and simple? Does complex language, vocabulary and syntax make it difficult for babies to learn? One easy way to think about it is what we call "The Great Preschool Television Schism." There are many approaches to speaking to babies and toddlers. *Blue's Clues* is the prime example of speaking as simply as possible, at a child's level. (Once upon a time, this was the method employed by *Mr. Rogers' Neighborhood*, for those of you working on childhood memories, not current information.) *Sesame*

Street is the prime example of including a more enriched subtext, although over the years, lamentably, the show has simplified its approach.

Let's look at some examples. Steve and Blue are always in expository mode. They are collecting and sifting information, engaging in make-believe dialogue (it can't be a real dialogue, since television is ultimately not interactive) with the viewer. Steve and Blue don't make side jokes. There is nothing included that is not accessible to the three-to-five-year-old. The show can only be enjoyed by an adult as a bizarre absurdist ritual. It's funny in the same way as watching those "English as a Second Language" vignettes in which two people speak to each other in a weirdly repetitive, elliptical dialogue (to fit the pedagogic needs): "Can I have the magazine?" "Which magazine do you want?" "I would like that magazine." "Is this the magazine you would like?"

Sesame Street, on the other hand, has always been full of characters, dialogue and situations that are every bit as entertaining for adults as they are for kids. There are parodies like "The O-kla-homa! Sketch," songs like "Rubber Ducky" or "I Love Trash" and comedic devices like Cookie Monster's voracity, Oscar's sardonicism, even Big Bird's innocent misinterpretations. Kids can enjoy them, but surely there are elements and side jokes, and subtexts that couldn't possibly make sense to them, and which have been added only to make the show pleasurable for adults. This is important for two reasons. First, because it adds a realistic layer of meaning for

kids to wrestle with. The world is full of references and subtexts. It is a more accurate view of the world, and better parallels the problem-solving and assigning of meanings that they will have to accomplish in the real world. Second, these elements make the show more interesting for the adults who are creating it and for the adults who are watching it. Show creators—writers, lyricists, puppeteers—who are making something that interests them, are more likely to create something that has real energy and power; as opposed to something that is educationally sound, but lifeless. The same thing goes for the adults who are watching TV with their young charges. A show that interests and amuses Mom is much more likely to have sustained interest for a toddler. After all, TV should ideally be a social activity.

All this is not to say that *Blues Clues* does not have its place. Steve, like Mr. Rogers before him, is a voice that kids absolutely trust and adore. The learning philosophy is no doubt sound. The repetition no doubt allows kids to analyze and understand the story. The open question is whether those goals must be met at the exclusion of other levels of interest. Finally, there is the very real possibility that while *Blues Clues* and other shows that remain always on a toddler's level of comprehension are good for kids, they may actually diminish the mental capacity of adults who are forced to watch them. This danger is not to be scoffed at.

What to Be Terrified About in the Toddler Years

BAD INFLUENCES

It was made for headlines. A sociologist presents research that demonstrates that parents are not the most important influence on their children. Genetics comes first, then peers, and parents place a poor third. Actually, the research also showed that Barney had as much influence as many parents.

All right, maybe the last part wasn't true, but the rest is. Now we may not have a Ph.D., and we're certainly not going to attempt to question anyone's methodology, but we sure are going to question the conclusions. After all, if it weren't for parents, who would turn happy two-year-olds into anal retentive bundles of neuroses? At whom would four-year-olds scream "I hate you?" Who would sixth graders pretend not to know? Who would teenagers rebel against? If it weren't for parents, what would anyone talk about in therapy? So have no fear, all your efforts as a parent will be amply rewarded.

But we're still left with the terrifying possibility that the random assortment of kids down at the preschool is going to have a large influence on your child's development. Whatever the percentages, there is no denying that your child's peers will have some influence, starting now and continuing throughout childhood.

You read food labels. You filter your drinking water. You checked your home for radon, asbestos, carbon monoxide. But how are you going to filter out the brats, whiners, manipulators and demon seeds as they toddle around the room? That one in the smock—could he be teaching your child that hitting is a good way of intimidating other children into giving up their toys? How about that one with the runny nose, he probably likes to play shooting games. That girl there looks like a classic whiner. Is that any kind of role model?

The fact is that entering into a social setting like preschool is just another important stage of learning. Just as you had to let baby fall a few times when learning to walk, and had to let baby make a mess when learning to use a spoon, you're going to have to watch your toddler make mistakes, get hurt, and figure out what makes other kids tick. All you can do is talk them through it. You can't keep Damian away from your child, you have to talk about why he behaves the way he does and what your child can do about it. That way you can inject an editorial subtext—and it doesn't have to be subtle. You might say—"Damian hits because he doesn't know how to use his words" or "Sometimes people who are sad inside, act mad on the outside" or "Sometimes there is born into the world pure evil." You'll just have to assess each situation on its own.

A FEW THINGS TO SAY
LET HER KNOW THAT YOU ARE
CARING, SENSITIVE AND UP ON THE
REQUIRED READING

Of course, you should be aware that the impression of being "caring and sensitive" will wear off quickly if you ask her to stop talking because you're watching the half-time show.

1. "Preschoolers have only recently gained a sense of self, so with that can come an exaggerated fear of injuries, because even minor problems represent a threat to their very existence. Scrapes and cuts can result in terror. For much the same reasons, this is the age at which children go through more adhesive bandages than any other. They simply have to have the blood covered up."

2. "Three- and four-year-olds have perhaps 500 words in their usable vocabulary. But in an average day, as they enjoy using their newfound ability to communicate, they will speak as many as 20,000 words! In other words (you wish!) they will be repeating themselves frequently, which can inevitably be irritating. But bear with it because it's important work they are doing."

3. "Try to save 'no' for the important rules and directions. Otherwise, you may find yourself saying it constantly, and it can become a habit. Instead, try answering suggestions with counter-suggestions, or just cut right to the explanation of why not. And of course, it's always fun to be wild now and then, and just say 'yes.' If you want to crack up a four-year-old, let them start their bath with all their clothes on. The clothes will dry out, and they're headed for the laundry anyway."

CHAPTER FOURTEEN

Childhood and Beyond

WHAT YOUR ABOVE-AVERAGE CHILD MAY BE DOING

• Still able to track object held close to the face

• Can say "Mom" and "Dad" but now in a long, drawn-out way that bespeaks embarrassment, resentment and frustration

• Beating you at chess

• Asking where babies come from, but just because he knows it will make you squirm

• Handicapping the horses with some success

• Ability to surf channels effectively, and use a VCR

• Showing an awareness of gender differences, and that there is something interesting about it

• Getting "tracked" into the "red" reading group

• Developing an intricate system of canvassing the neighborhood that allows for the absolute maximum take of Halloween candy

• Learning to fake happiness and appreciation when gifts are presented

• Questioning your moral relativism, i.e. "If it's the speed limit, isn't it illegal to go over it?" and "Why did you tell Aunt Martha we were going to the movies?"

• Demanding things based on the "all the other kids get to" argument

• Using reverse psychology on a friend

• Sending e-mail

• Resenting his siblings

WHAT YOUR WIFE MAY BE COMPLAINING ABOUT

• Exhaustion

• You

• That you should have thought more carefully about when you conceived because your child's birth date makes him the youngest/oldest kid in his grade

• Your reluctance to have a vasectomy

• Gray hair

• Girls' self-esteem issues

• Boys' violent and competitive tendencies

• The TV shows you used to enjoy are now so inappropriate and full of suggestive jokes, negative stereotyping and rudeness

• The high cost of education

• Your household toys, games and crafts intake—from relatives, holidays, birthdays—is so intense that by the time your child is six you have a shelf devoted entirely to things that still have the shrink-wrap on them

• They grow up so fast

What You May Be Concerned About
NAMING REDUX

"This may sound crazy, but we're thinking about having another baby. We figure that as long as the house is a disaster area, we're still not even sleeping that late, and there is always a funny smell somewhere, we might as well provide the sibling every child deserves. What should we be worried about?"

There are, naturally, many challenges that face parents who are about to embark on the adventure that is a second child. Certainly, they can expect no sympathy from their only child, whose world is about to be shaken to the core. As some wise advisor once suggested, there isn't much point trying to explain to your first child that there is plenty of love to go around. Put yourself in his place. "Honey, you're a great husband and I love you so much, I've decided to get another husband, too. This is Phil. Phil, Bob. Bob, Phil."

These matters of sorting through the issues of sibling rivalry are too complex to cover in any detail. We could probably write a book on it, and probably will, given half a chance. But there is one important task that we should address before another tragic mistake is made. You will need to choose a name for the second child, and now you have all the same factors that made choosing the first name so complicated and time-consuming, plus the special ingredient: you need a name that won't sound odd or too cute with the first child's name. Here are some problem areas.

Rhyming. Phil and Lil works for the Rugrats, but not in real life.

Word play. Adam and Amanda is just too cute. So is Anne and Andy. And if you were considering Pete and Petunia, you're on your own.

Alliteration. Why threaten your children's sense of individuality by going with Josie and Jack, Kevin and Kora, David and Danielle? Why not give them their own initials?

Famous Couples. Sam and Dave. Steve and Edie. Peter, Paul and Mary. The jokes will get old fast.

Television. It's a great source of entertainment, but not of names (don't name your kid Felicity!) or name combinations. Sam and Diane, Jerry and Elaine, Drew and Mimi. These will all be in reruns for decades to come.

What You May Be Concerned About
THE BIRDS AND THE BEES

"Okay, I've seen the PSAs. I think I can do the drugs talk, and the smoking kills talk, but I don't really have to have the birds and the bees talk, do I?"

Nope. Kids today are born knowing all about human sexuality. You'll be fine never mentioning it.

What You May Be Concerned About

LITTLE LEAGUE

"I guess I'm kind of a frustrated athlete, played a lot of sports back in school. My wife says I shouldn't even be allowed near little league sports, but I'm sure I'll be able to handle it when the time comes."

Forget about it. Even parents who have no interest in sports, and are only involved because their kid is so "active" and "well-coordinated," can lose control of themselves in the face of competitive sports. All the talk about doing your best and having fun goes out the window as the spectators/parents let their frustration build until it bursts out in inappropriate behavior ranging from haranguing their own kid—"No, no, no...the other way, the goal is the other way"—to ranting about the lousy referee (no doubt a fellow member of the PTA who is just trying to help out and only learned the rules of soccer three weeks ago at a half-hour "clinic.")

Baseball, soccer, hockey, football, gymnastics, it's all the same. Ordinary, civilized, polite parents are suddenly transformed into powder kegs. Why is it? There are two answers, both of which are contributing factors. First is the sideline.

There it is: a line you cannot cross. Your child is out there; you're over here. You can't kick the ball, pick up a grounder, or turn a handspring for him. He is on his own. Whether you were all-state or picked last in gym class, you can probably play soccer significantly better than the average seven-year-old, and the desire to run out on the field and do it simmers below the surface.

The second major contributing factor is related. Nowhere in our modern culture is success and failure so clearly delineated. Competition is politically incorrect, so we live in denial. We keep repeating the truisms of good sportsmanship: doing your best, fair play, etc., etc. In school, in the playground, there are different activities for different kids, but there are very few winners and losers. Grade evaluations have been renamed and defanged until everybody seems to be satisfactory. My kid is okay, and your kid is okay. We're all okay.

Then the kids hit the soccer field, or the diamond, or the swimming pool. And guess what? It turns out my kid is actually better than yours, faster than yours, better suited to play shortstop than yours. Or vice versa. In any case, there is no denying it. Success and failure are no longer a matter of relative effort and subjective opinion. Watching this drama unfold is too much for most parents. The thrill of victory and agony of defeat lead inevitably to parents making fools of themselves.

Can it be avoided? You must recognize the enemy. Knowing that you care too much is the first step. Try to focus on how stupid other parents who are yelling at their kids sound. Keep repeating that you're here so your kid can have fun. Finally, if you feel that you can't take it and are likely to end up doing something stupid, join a team. That's right, go down to the YMCA or community center and sign up for softball or volleyball or whatever you enjoy. But it has to be a competitive sport. Recreational swimming won't do it. Playing a sport of your own will do three things. First, it will serve as an outlet for your competitive fire. Second, it may remind you that it's not so easy performing in the arena. Third, you'll see that it really can be fun, win or lose. And try to hold that thought. Or rent *Bad News Bears* again.

What It's Important to Know

THE PRE-REBELLION YEARS

As a relatively new father, your main concern is bonding with your child, drawing him close, nurturing and protecting him. Now you've got to spend the rest of his childhood undoing all that. That's right, once you have your toddler fully trained in the fine art of dependence, total trust, and unquestioning affection, you must begin the work of teaching him independence, judgment, and affection with discretion.

Maybe you don't want to look ahead, and start dreading childhood and (gasp!) the teenager! This is not the fun part of parenting. You'll have to let your two-year-old jump into the sandbox from the side over and over, just knowing that eventually he is going to land on his face. But how else can he learn to jump? You'll watch him tumble, scrape, and bang. You'll watch him get pushed around by bullies. You'll compliment artwork that you both know doesn't look much like what it was intended to be. You'll watch him strike out and hang his head. You'll suffer through homework, unfair teachers, impossible assignments. A lot of failure goes into every success.

The worst part is that you sometimes have to be the bad guy. Learning about independence, and rules, and authority means testing limits. Yeah, limits you set and enforce. You won't be perfect. You'll be grumpy some days, hand out unwarranted punishments, yell about nothing at all one day, and laugh it all off the next. Learning that people don't always react the same way is an important lesson in itself.

You might think now you're always going to be your kid's best friend, but you can't be. Kids need something to rebel against. Like it or not, one of your most important roles is to provide a system of beliefs that your child can analyze, critique, dismiss, and, you hope, one day return to. You hope that they can keep it down to hating your music, your hair and your occasional hypocrisy, and still want to have dinner with you. So long as the lines of communication are open, there is positive work being done. Throughout it all, and it may sometimes be hard to believe, you have to remember that the highly charged criticism, the doubtful snipes, the sullen resentment, even the rebellious anger, all stem from the fact that ultimately yours really is the opinion that matters most to them.

THAT YOU WERE A BAD PARENT

Oh, maybe it was a face of despair you made during toilet training. Maybe it was that time you weren't watching and your baby tumbled off the sofa like a train wreck. Maybe it was when you lost your temper and yelled that it was your two-year-old's fault that the Broncos lost. You'll probably never know exactly when, or what it was, but somewhere along the way, you scarred your child for life.

That's right. People make mistakes in all walks of life, but only mistakes in parenting (and plastic surgery, I suppose) automatically "scar for life." Eventually, your children will learn to live with the psychic wounds your inadequate parenting has inflicted on them, some with more therapy than others. Should you feel guilty? Most therapy in the United States is basically a process of looking back and figuring out how wrong your parents were and accepting how angry with them you are. However, in Japan psychotherapy is generally a process by which you explore your childhood experience and learn to ask for your parents' forgiveness for all that you did wrong. Go figure.

So you can feel guilty, or feel unappreciated. Or you will alternate between both. There are no perfect kids and no perfect parents. You do what you can, and the best advice is simply to give parenting your all. Be there for your kids. Spend the time to get to know them. Cherish the things that go right. Laugh at the things that go wrong. Sure, work is important, but keep everything in perspective. As popular wisdom puts it, no one ever reflected back on their life and thought, "I wish I had spent more time at the office." On the other hand, it's probably just as true that no one ever reflected back and thought, "Boy, if I could just go back and give one more 2 A.M. feeding."

Happy parenting!